# THE
# RUSS
# & JONO
## BREAKFAST EXPERIENCE

*The publishers are especially grateful to Richard Topping,*
*without whose contribution this book would not be what it is.*

First published in Great Britain in 1997 by
Virgin Publishing
332 Ladbroke Grove
London W10 5AH

Text copyright © Russ Williams and Jonathan Coleman 1997

Additional text by Richard Topping

Pictures supplied by Virgin Radio, Rex Features, All Action,
Retna, Collections, PA News, Mirror Syndication International,
Universal, Pictorial Press, Agency Ltd.

A catalogue record for this book is available from the British Library.

ISBN 0 7535 0123 6

Designed by Blackjacks, London
Reproduction by Scanners

Printed by Bookprint, Spain

# THE RUSS & JONO
## BREAKFAST EXPERIENCE

Virgin

*Welcome to the Russ & Jono Breakfast Experience and congratulations! You're a winner! That's right. Just by the very act of walking into your local literary outlet and buying this book you have taken your very first step along the road to Instant Success!*

But wait. Don't get complacent and start awarding yourself 75% pay rises already. You've got some work to do. 96 pages of work, in fact, for this tome is not just another fly-by-night-cash-in-concept thrown together over a drunken lunch five minutes before the print deadline. No, it's much more than that. It is a carefully thought-out, fully time-managed bible for those who watch others gorge at the trough of success and say to themselves 'I'm a big, fat, greedy pig, too. Where's my bag of slurry?'

You can't be good at everything – some of us can't be good at anything – but no matter which field of endeavour may leave you feeling 'virginal', the *Russ & Jono Breakfast Experience Virgin Guides* contained within these elaborately designed pages will guarantee you Instant Success!

But what gives us the right to tell you how to become Instantly Successful? Just take a look at the intimate behind-the-scenes glimpses of our award-winning wireless show. Fifteen hard years of slogging our way slowly but surely up the greasy pole, that is. And now that we've arrived at the summit and become Instantly Successful we can finally turn round and toss a rope ladder down to a few, closely selected-millions beneath us.

No book as wide ranging and as sexually fulfilling as this, however, could have been completed without some kind of help and we would like to take this opportunity to express our grateful thanks to the following who contributed so much to the Instant Success of this work: Wolfgang Amadeus Mozart, Lady Olga Maitland, Dr Hilary Jones, Bobby Crush, Jeanette Winterton, The Magpie Team – especially Tommy Boyd – Casper Weinberger, DJ Kat, Martin Amis, The Moscow State Circus (both companies), Vanessa Feltz, Tony Benn, Tommy Steele, Stephen King, Jonathan King and King Juan Carlos of Spain, Cornelius Agrippa, Eddie The Eagle, Alastair Stewart and Fiona Foster – thank you very much indeed, Zoe Ball and Andi Peters, Aesculyus, Sophocles and the rest of the Greek back four and finally Harry the cab driver who said "'Ere. Why don't you two wankers do a f\*\*ng book?".

*Russ and Jono – The Breakfast Brothers – with their biggest fans.*

# That's My Boy

## A TIPTOE THROUGH
## MRS SYLVIA COLEMAN'S PHOTO ALBUM

They say a star is born and not made and it came as no surprise to me that my little Jonathan should choose this method of coming into the world. The happy event took place on the 29th of February 1956 in a small cottage hospital in Hackney, East London when the sounds of Bow bells a-belling and chirpy market traders a-trading was drowned out by the cry of a little pink person falling from his mummy's tummy into this world – and just in time for lunch too. As soon as the vittles appeared he was as quiet and content as a pig in nappies – which, strangely enough, was what the midwife said he looked like too.

From day one little Johnny loved his grub and was more than happy to eat whatever was put in front of him, including two small teddies and a metal blanket-bath bowl. The poor little nurses could hardly keep up with him and his little bawled orders for this or that menu. To this day Jonathan still has a special affection for nurses. In fact only the other week someone from *The Sun* rang up and told me he'd been paying some nice young student to dress up as one and give him a blanket bath at her flat in Maida Vale. Isn't that the sweetest thing you've ever heard? He really is such a poppet.

To be quite honest, Jonathan's babyhood is all a bit of a blur to me now as, very soon after his birth, he was rushed off to the National Atomic Laboratory in Mill Hill for a series of top-secret tests. The next time I saw him he was quite grown up for a two-year-old. He had a shock of bright-red hair, a deep voice and all his own teeth (and a few of someone else's too). He also had managed to grow a large moustache which I thought was very dashing. Unfortunately his father, who'd had a regrettable encounter with an RAF officer when he was a lad, thought otherwise and he cropped it off that very day with his Spear & Jackson shears. To be honest I was more worried about the fact that his skin was bright orange until my good friend Beryl pointed out that those lovely kids on the Ready Brek ad had it too, and so it must be perfectly normal.

From quite early on my husband Maurice and I knew that Jonathan was very different from his big sister Sharon. He wasn't interested in Action Man or tractors or Rugby League. He lived and breathed one thing and one thing only – ponies. Oh yes, I can almost see him now prising himself into his jodhpurs and heading off to the Southgate Guides Gymkhana to hang around the horse boxes with the other little girls and try to get a ride.

I don't when it was that my husband and I first realised that Jonathan was 'theatrical' but certainly by the age of seven or so he left us in no doubt about his leanings. His first performances were musical ones. In fact he had the rare ability after certain spicy meals to use his whole body like an instrument. I don't think any of us will ever forget the solo rendition he gave of the eruption of Mount Vesuvius after we'd had curried beans on toast for tea.

Soon enough, though, Jonathan got into acting. He spent hours at Clovelly Beach playing that part of John Mills directing the Normandy landings in *The Longest Day* – or at least that's what he said he was doing when he was staring at the ladies' chests and muttering something about 'damned fine inflatables'. Unfortunately his school play career was cut tragically short soon after this when he took things a little too far in a production of *The Rape Of The Sabine Women* and upset the nuns.

Jonathan was always a very funny, if somewhat clumsy, child. Hardly a day would go by without him having us all in stitches, and himself too, particularly when he was working on that wacky lawn-mower routine of his. Luckily, after a time Jonathan got so used to

seeing the doctors sewing him back together with a needle and thread that he was able to do it himself. This worked very well until his needlework teacher at school introduced him to crochet which just didn't hold the bits in quite as well as a decent box stitch.

In 1965 our lives took a bit of a different turn when, right out of the blue, one day my husband announced that we were going for a spin out to the Norholt War Memorial in the Austin A40 and took us instead to Sydney, Australia where he'd heard they were doing Watney's Red Barrel at sixpence a pint. Of course it was all a little strange at first though I quickly settled when I found that they too had a local branch of Woolies and repeats of *Crossroads* on the telly.

Jonathan took to his new life like a duck to water. Within a couple of hours he had a nice strong Australian accent, a tinny in each hand and could tell the colour of a young girl's underwear at fifty paces. School life was a bit of a shock to him as they were much more keen on discipline over there than they were back in Southgate. Here he is (above left) receiving six of the best from Brad the head boy for unauthorised use of Brad's best diamanté bicycle shorts. As you can see, Jonathan is, as usual, trying to cover his shame and embarrassment with a smile.

As a teenager Jonathan went through a rebellious phase, growing his hair long and being rude to his distant relatives on the phone. Luckily this only lasted for one afternoon and he was soon back to his normal happy-go-lucky self, borrowing his sister's clothes to go to discos and meeting up with his Maths master for extra lessons in the local park toilets. Come to think of it, Jonathan always seemed to get very good marks from Mr Philpotts even when he didn't show all his working out. He must have been a clever little devil in his own way.

Here he is (above right) launching his journalistic career as editor of a magazine modestly entitled the *Voice Of Young Australia* or *Voya* for short. Though Jonathan did explain to me that Voyeurism was less a journal and more a way of life I never could quite see the appeal of staying up late in smoky offices with lots of young female student journalists looking at pictures of celebrities caught with their clothes off. Then again I never was one for intellectual magazines myself.

This is Jonathan (right) as a first-year student at the Military Academy of Queensland – a finishing school for the privileged few that destiny has picked out

as future leaders of this great country of ours. It was his father's idea to send him there and though he initially resisted the idea he soon came round when he realised he would get to wear thigh-length riding boots and carry his very own whip. The fact that he was thrown out the second day for dancing during drill practice was, of course, a big disappointment to us all but I know that to this day the experience stood him in good stead – particularly in his political conversations with that nice Gary Bushell bloke on his radio programme.

As he got bigger (and bigger and bigger) even our permanent staff at seventeen centres couldn't cope with his healthy boy's appetite and here he is (above) rustling up his own *Breakfast Experience* on the barbie – a dozen sausages, four chops, two chickens and a tomato.

As for Jonathan's meteoric rise to fame I can say very little as we don't get British radio down under. By the way, if you see my little Johnny-boy, tell him I said hello and that a phone call would be nice once in a while. Even though I enjoy those little chats with his lawyer I'd quite like to have a one-to-one natter with him about something other than the terms of my will.

Must stop now as all this writing is giving me cramp. If only the nurse would give me my own set of keys to these bloomin' handcuffs . . .

*Sylvia Coleman*

# Probe the

Some lovers just don't know when to stop in pursuit of their amorous quests. One young Romeo – André Schmidt from Moers, Germany – was so keen to see the object of his desires that he started six million quid's worth of fires just so that he could get her hubby – one of the town's firemen – out of the way. Unfortunately the plan backfired when his paramour, a shapely Frau called Bettina, was so impressed by her husband's heroic deeds that she refused André's advances, claiming she'd fallen back in love with her brave hubby.

All beer served at Fat Eddie's bar in Toronto, Canada, every Tuesday night is free – until, that is, someone goes to the loo. As soon as the first person wees, Eddie's prices go straight back up to normal. The weak-bladdered customer than has to wear a T-shirt that says, 'I wrecked the party.'

A pretty 25-year-old Spanish teacher went to her local doctor in Malaga following a minor car accident to check for concussion and discovered that she was suffering from a condition previously unknown to medical science – breast whiplash. The doctor ordered her to strip and then proceeded to fondle and stroke her breasts for nearly quarter of an hour. When questioned by police, the naughty medic said, 'Breasts are very wonderful and delicate things. Anything that can happen to a neck can easily happen to them.' Reports that actress Lesley Joseph was seen at Gatwick Airport boarding a flight for Malaga were later found to be completely untrue.

# Globe

Some cabbies turn up late. Some overcharge. Some bore you to death with their bigoted and blinkered views. Few have quite the style however to get their passengers to do the driving. Argentinean cabbie Carlos Silvera does just that however and, on the entirely reasonable grounds that he's getting old and his eyesight isn't what it once was, makes his customers take the wheel while he sits in the back and smokes himself to death.

Former porn star Claudia Pinelli has found a new career – publishing girlie magazines and running a series of perverted sex phone lines. During a recent testimony to an Italian Government committee on public morals, she claimed her lines received more than 100,000 calls a week. When pressed by an MP to describe just what sort of sick-minded people used her service, Claudia produced a spread-sheet full of very precise figures. Of all the calls she received, over 3,000 came from Italian Government offices, 15,000 came from the HQ of the Italian Army and nearly 1,000 came from within the walls of the Vatican.

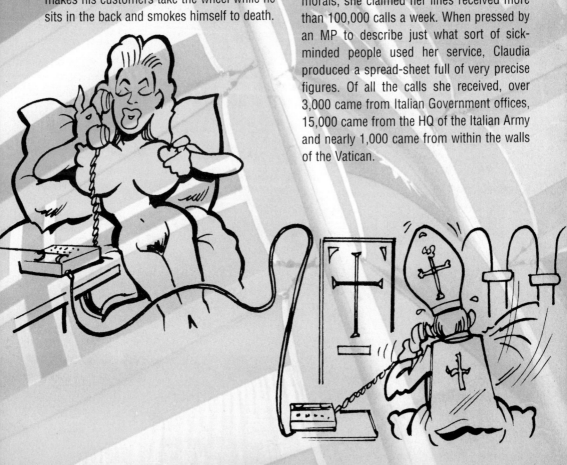

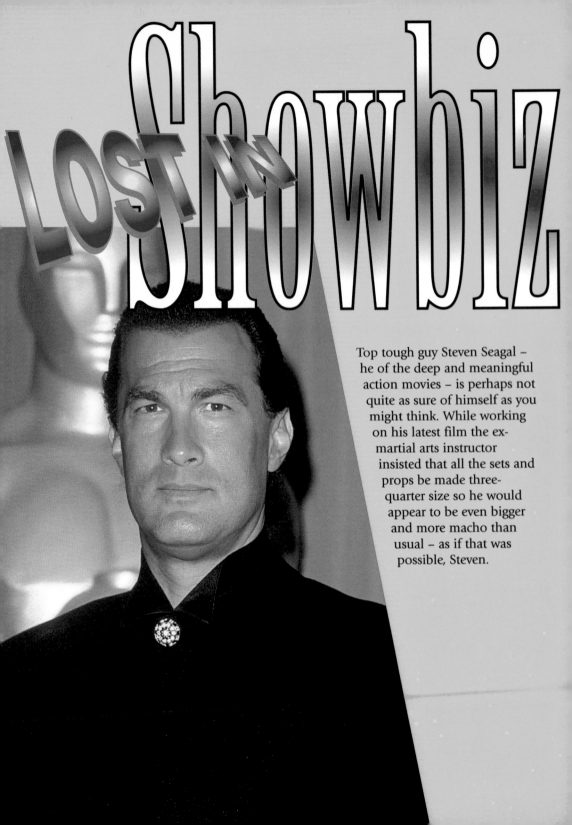

# LOST IN Showbiz

Top tough guy Steven Seagal – he of the deep and meaningful action movies – is perhaps not quite as sure of himself as you might think. While working on his latest film the ex-martial arts instructor insisted that all the sets and props be made three-quarter size so he would appear to be even bigger and more macho than usual – as if that was possible, Steven.

# Hey kids, here's the chance you've all been waiting for – your chance to go to ...

# Wank
# in Germany

*The impressive Chataeux Von Wank*

### That's right. Wank – a charming village high in the German Alps, not far from the world-famous religious festival town of Oberammergau.

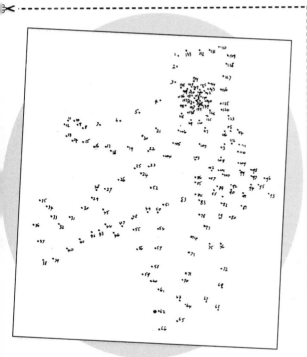

All you have to do to earn your chance to win this fabulous prize is study the image on the left and join the dots to reveal a picture of a well-known, lovable, bearded multi-millionaire British tycoon. Once you've joined all the dots you simply have to use your skill and imagination to add that special something to Richard Branson. It could be another person, an extra appendage or two, or even an everyday household item.

The judges will be looking for style, inventiveness, wit and some seriously twisted minds. The decision of the judges will be final.

*'I've been to Wank in Germany and loved every minute of it.'* - JUDITH CHARMERS

*'Despite stiff competition, I'd go to Wank in Germany before I'd go anywhere else.'* - MAJOR RONALD FERGIESON

*'The Wankers were very friendly as Wankers go.'* - GARY BUSHELL

## DON'T DELAY - GET DRAWING TODAY

# Wank
# Competition

Mr/Mrs/Miss/Ms.......... Initials................

Surname................................................

Address................................................

.............................................................

Postcode................................................

**The Small Print:** If your eyesight is still good enough to read this, you're not going to Wank. This entire page is composed around one dodgy joke based on the unfortunately named town of Wank. Even if you're desperate to come, and send us large amounts of cash in small denominations, or unmarked, used notes which cannot be returned under any circumstances, we can't get you to Wank. If you've already whipped out your pencil and pulled off a personal best on the dot-to-dot, we suggest you just toss it.

Environment news now. The Ukrainian government has turned down a financial aid package to help pay for their efforts to deal with the remaining radiation at Chernobyl. The Ukrainians explained their actions by saying they prefer to stand on their own three feet.

Thank you very much indeed.

European news just in off the wires. A French women faces the death penalty after murdering her husband for constantly farting throughout their twenty-year marriage. Legal sources say she might well get the gas chamber.

A man trapped in a superloo as it went through its 25-minute self-cleaning cycle was soaked to the skin and threatened to sue the manufacturers today for damage to his clothes and the loss of his *Daily Mirror* which he hadn't even finished.

TORY PARTY WORKER REG SHRUB RUSHED HIS YOUNGEST CHILD TO HOSPITAL TODAY WHEN HE REALISED THAT THE POOR CHILD HAD EATEN AN ENTIRE COPY OF THE TORY'S LAST ELECTION MANIFESTO, BUT WAS TURNED AWAY FROM THE HOSPITAL BY DOCTORS WHO SAID, 'DON'T BE DAFT, NOBODY EVER SWALLOWED THAT CRAP.'

**Royal news now. The Duchess of York was caught in a traffic jam today when roads protestors blocked the highway. When asked what she felt about roads, Her Royal Fergieness replied, 'Rhodes is very nice but I prefer Corfu at this time of year.'**

**Thank You Very Much Indeed.**

## EDWARD & SHANKA'S

# BEST OF THE NEWS HEADLINES

NEWS JUST IN . . . BIG BEN IS SET TO STAR IN NEW TV AD FOR JAMAICAN CONDOMS.
Thank you very much indeed

The Prime Minister Tony Blair was in Brussels yesterday. Asked whether he though Britain needed a new agriculture programme for the late 90s Mr Blair said, 'No . . . Emmerdale will do just fine.'

The world of classical music was in shock today as experts reveal that Mozart suffered from Tourettes Syndrome – the disease which cause people to say swear words uncontrollably in the most unlikely circumstances. At last scholars have the explanation for Mozart's Symphony in F Off Major.

TYCOON RICHARD BRANSON IS RECOVERING TODAY AFTER COLLAPSING FROM HEAT EXHAUSTION DURING A TRIP TO THE CARIBBEAN. DES O' CONNOR SAYS THE SAME THING HAPPENS TO HIM IF HE SUNBATHES FOR MORE THAN 10 MONTHS AT A TIME.
Thank you very much indeed

NEW YORK POLICE HAVE BECOME INVOLVED IN A SPECIAL CHRISTMAS PROMOTION. WHEN YOU GET ARRESTED YOU CAN HAVE YOUR MUG SHOT TAKEN SITTING ON SANTA'S LAP. Thank you very much indeed.

chided him that the least he could have done was send me a postcard he said he had. The card had crossed 78 trillion billion miles of space in a nanosecond before falling into the hands of the Royal Mail who had taken thirteen years, eleven months and 28 days to deliver it. Coincidentally, the very day after Russ walked back in with four hundredweight of dirty washing, the postcard arrived. Life really can be strange sometimes.

Of course I'm very proud of Russ and his new life as a top radio and TV personality and hardly a day goes by when I don't tune into Radio 1 and enjoy his wacky japes and off-the-wall northern humour. I do worry sometimes about Russ having to mix with a lower class of person as part of his showbiz duties. He has never had much of a head for alcohol and his friendly, open nature means that he's easily led astray by unscrupulous types who want to dip their beaker in his cup of fame.

On the right you can see the unfortunate result of Russ's attempt to pass his entire head through his granny's mangle. I believe it's all popped back into shape now . . . apart from the ears.

I hope and pray that Russ never gets involved in any scandals though this is unlikely as the only time he's ever got frisky in that way was during the 1970 World Cup when England scored against Brazil and he made a bit of a mess against Uncle Cyril's trouser leg. Luckily Cyril was wearing his fawn polyester slacks and they came up lovely in the wash or there could have been a bit of a scene.

Of course my photo-album isn't quite complete yet. There's one big space in it that I'm keeping for a little, special event that every mother dreams about. That's right. I know it's a bit naughty of me but I can't help dropping hints to my boy about when I can expect to hear the patter of tiny feet. Still, I'm sure that Russ will meet Ronnie Corbett one day.

*Patricia Primrose Williams*

down the front of his shorts – at least that's what he told me happened. From that moment on he was hooked, though it took him a few years to go from from belting out hits from the shows in fishnet stockings to his true calling as a top radio and TV personality.

This is Russ making his first ever professional appearance when he opened the school fete with those two lovely twins from *Neighbours* (they wandered off just as I was lining up this shot). Of course they've gone on to much greater things now but I'm sure they'd recognise Russ anywhere if he were still wearing his special red sandals.

I'll always treasure the memory of my little boy going off to school in his first school uniform. I only wish it was the right one for his school and not something he stole from the boy next door who went to private tutorial college down the road. From that point on he only referred to me as Mater and insisted on being punished by getting me to thrash him to within an inch of his life. Bless him.

Unfortunately Russ's teenage years are a bit of a mystery to me as one summer's day in 1975 he went out to buy to buy a copy of *Whizzer and Chips* and some Action Transfers and didn't come back for fourteen years. Far from being trapped at the back of an especially long queue at Smith's as we had thought, Russ had in fact been abducted by a far-off alien race called the Hagues (see page 38). These strange and barbarous people took poor little Russ away to a galaxy 45,000 light years away and force fed him on a diet of satellite TV, football and Silk Cut Extra Mild. When I

dropping ice cream down the front of ladies' bikinis. It was on the beach that he met his best holiday friend who later grew up to be the Arsenal captain, Tony Adams. Young Tony had a great influence on my boy and shaped his football thinking with his fascinating insights into how the game should really be played – which is why to this day Russ still supports Tottenham United.

From a very early age Russ knew that he wanted to go into show business. I think the real turning point came when he tuned into *Junior Showtime* and saw young Bonnie Langford perform 'The Pineapple Song' from *Cabaret* with Neil Reid. He got so excited that he spilt half his Corona Cream Soda

# That's My Boy

## A TIPTOE THROUGH
## MRS PATRICIA PRIMROSE WILLIAMS' PHOTO ALBUM

Russ was born into this world on the 21st of January 19 hundred and 62. It was a Wednesday I think. The weather was a little cold and damp in the morning though it did freshen up nicely after *Wagonners' Walk.* I don't know why, call me psychic, but as soon as I got up that morning I just knew that today I was going to have a baby – which was doubly strange as at that moment I didn't even know I was pregnant. After all, there have been cases of indigestion that lasted nine months before, surely?

Anyway, whatever the moral rights and wrongs, around four o'clock that afternoon I came over all queer at the launderette and had to be revived with a nice cup of Typhoo and a couple of thick slices of Battenburg. Three hours later little Russ came into this world, naked but for his Spurs scarf and a large rosette with Glenn Hoddle's face on it. He didn't scream when the midwife slapped his bottom, only when she stopped. Babies can be strange creatures sometimes.

From the start Russ stood out from the crowd. He was always cheerful, friendly and immensely self-confident – though his habit of leaning out of his pram and handing out signed pictures of himself was a bit of a nuisance when I was trying to scoot round Spar and get back in time for *Pebble Mill.* Unfortunately I missed Russ's first words as I was upstairs in the bedroom at the time having a private chat with that nice, handsome washing machine man but I'm sure they were as funny as he said they were.

Time flies by when you've got a baby to look after and so many catalogues to study and suddenly one day I looked up from the Green Shield Stamps' hostess trolley selection to find him dressed and ready to go to school. Unfortunately this was on a Sunday in August so he had a little longer before he could turn the sandpit into a no-fly zone and start teaching his classmates to look out for the smutty bits in *Captain Pugwash.*

Russ loved his holidays, especially those happy, happy weeks at Blackpool when he had so much fun pouring boiling oil down from the turret of his impregnable sand castles and

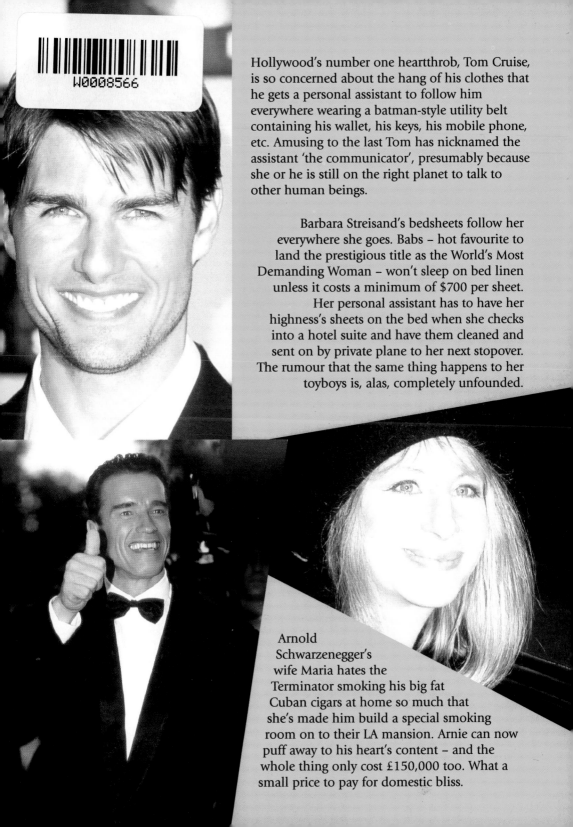

Hollywood's number one heartthrob, Tom Cruise, is so concerned about the hang of his clothes that he gets a personal assistant to follow him everywhere wearing a batman-style utility belt containing his wallet, his keys, his mobile phone, etc. Amusing to the last Tom has nicknamed the assistant 'the communicator', presumably because she or he is still on the right planet to talk to other human beings.

Barbara Streisand's bedsheets follow her everywhere she goes. Babs – hot favourite to land the prestigious title as the World's Most Demanding Woman – won't sleep on bed linen unless it costs a minimum of $700 per sheet. Her personal assistant has to have her highness's sheets on the bed when she checks into a hotel suite and have them cleaned and sent on by private plane to her next stopover. The rumour that the same thing happens to her toyboys is, alas, completely unfounded.

Arnold Schwarzenegger's wife Maria hates the Terminator smoking his big fat Cuban cigars at home so much that she's made him build a special smoking room on to their LA mansion. Arnie can now puff away to his heart's content – and the whole thing only cost £150,000 too. What a small price to pay for domestic bliss.

# CURRICULUM VITAE

# *Russ Williams*

*Name:* RUSS Mullery Chivers Linekar
Gillzine Gascoigne Perryman Klinzman
Venables Ardiles Waddle Hoddle Jennings
(sub) WILLIAMS.

*Date of Birth:* 21/11/62

*Age:* 26
(on the Paula Yates showbiz-years scale)

*Address:*    c/o Director's Box
            Tottenham Hotspur Football Club
            High Road
            London
            N17

*Qualifications:* Too
many to mention.
Not only have I been
an avid fan of
David 'Diddy'
Hamilton for
many years but
more than two
of my mum's
friends have
said that I've
got a nice
voice and
should be
on the
radio.

*Education:* I have a number of educational qualifications that include BA, MA, PHD, RAC, BBC, ABTA, CNN, OBE, OFTEL and the back of my mother's hand.
'O' Levels – Erm... Does cooking count ?
'A' Levels – George Best's Soccer Skills, Lechery and Geography (Pure and Applied)
Degrees: Three
Tops: Four
And Mother Makes: Five

*Employment History:* Employment began way back in the dawn of time when the first known Boss crawled out of the primeval mud and started talking about teamwork, productivity and flexible working. Very soon after this . . . [Ed: All right, all right, we get the 'joke'.]

*Work Record:*
All The Day, All The Night – The Kinks
Working My Way Back To You Babe –
Let's Work – Mick Jagger
Jamming – Bob Marley
Blue Monday – New Order
Unfinished Sympathy – Massive Attack

*Jobs I Have Done*
1979 – 1988 – I broadened my horizons and sought new opportunities once every fortnight at the Job Centre, Baxley.
Sep 1988 – Dec 24 1988 – Provider of executive relief to major figures in the poultry industry (Turkey Wanker).
1989 – 1994 – Creator of Special Comedy material, Khmer Rouge People's Army in and around the jungles of the Burma/Laos border.

*Interests:* Film, music, dance, fine wine, the early novels of George Bernard Shaw, 16.5% non-controlling stake in the newly privatised Sewerage Inspectorate, UFOs, outing heterosexual happily-married politicians, Turkey Wanking and trying to imagine what all these gorgeous babes could possibly (allegedly) see in Chris Evans.

*Skills and Achievements:* I was head boy at all eleven of my former schools and would like to deny right here and now that I had anything at all to do with sticking those bangers up Fatty Jackson's arse. I consider myself to be a model citizen and a good father to my children – wherever they are. I don't want to boast but I've also been recently voted 'Man Most Likely To Succeed In Radio' at the annual Emma Freud Media Awards.

*Referees:* George Courtney, Clive Thomas, Clive Norling and that nice, tubby bloke with the dipstick on *It's A Knockout.*

You know people often ask me – OK, close relatives on my Mother's side – they say Chris, what do you wacky young DJ guys get up to while the records are playing? Well, at last the truth can be revealed as I unveil my secret list of just some of the important career-advancing Instantly Successful things myself and Russ get up to while a certain classic track is gracing our laser-heads. I think I feel a title coming on . . .

# 20 THINGS A HIGHLY PROFESSIONAL DJ CAN DO WHILE 'STAIRWAY TO HEAVEN' IS PLAYING

*. . . Ooo. That's better . . .*

LED ZEPPELIN

1 Do shopping – for yourself and elderly neighbours (try to keep to a five-mile radius to studio depending on traffic conditions and whether or not you've brought your string bag with you).

2 Get another haircut. Preferably the long, greying one growing out of your left nostril.

3 Phone Rolf Harris in Australian bush, hold phone up to speakers and inform him how much he's missing out on in royalties by you playing the original Led Zep version.

4 Make quick baguette-and-brioche-style picnic lunch, remembering to wash the lettuce and dead-head the radish.

5 Have very long soak in executive DJ bath using full range of Jane Seymour Fresh Body toiletries. Restage Battle Of Trafalgar using exact replica of Nelson's flagship *Victory* and yellow rubber duckie. Strangely this time the French win.

6 Locate and mend faint but irritating squeak on the back axle of Russ's 1984 canary-yellow Austin Allegro. Also make good damage to Dog Is For Life Not Just For Christmas sticker and re-bore mechanic with snaps of visit to Drag Racing at Castle Donnington.

7 Organise body-piercing session for yourself and work experience person of your choice, including travelling time and visit to accident and emergency unit of Charing Cross Hospital.

8 Nip down to British Library to study differences between first and second drafts of Shakespeare's *King Lear* to test pet theory that the Bard's plays were, in fact, actually written by Naomi Campbell. Why else would her excellent novel *Swan* be named after Shakespeare's very own theatre? (Ceefax page 889.)

9 Make slightly less quick baguette-and-brioche-style French lunch, remembering to marinate the *moules* in their own urine and not to spill too much of the brandy while you're pouring it on the paté. Use salt as recommended in Gary Rhodes's brilliant new book *Rhodes to Nowhere.*

10 Take a Virgin train to Fort William and wait for Northern Lights to come on. Return with two Norwegian girl hikers who believed your story about your strange friendship with the Duke Of Edinburgh.

11 Learn Norwegian – pure and applied.

12 Write, record and edit 26-part international TV series and short docu-drama about the life and times of Derek Nimmo.

13 Enjoy luxury Round The World Trip with Korean Airlines including day 84 life-threatening refuelling stop-over in New York and a fortnight all-expenses-paid sojourn in a no-go area in Somalia for co-pilot's niece's wedding.

14 Prepare full deluxe version of baguette-and-brioche-style French lunch, including hand-rearing own veal calves, creating new variety of aphrodisiac cucumbers and growing, making and maturing own wine using a blend of *pinot noir* and *grenache grapes,*

15 Same except for substituting *cabernet sauvignon* for *pinot noir* and using slightly more diet mayonnaise in the brown baps.

16 Record entire *Lord Of The Rings* trilogy for special slow-learners edition of Talking Books. Include all footnotes and extensive quotes from the most impossible passages of *The Silmarillion.*

17 stage and star in new rock opera with Andrew Lloyd Webber based on the life of Vanessa Feltz called *Old Tart With A TV Show.*

18 Start new art movement based in Bristol that involves mixing human saliva with toothpaste and smearing it – in the form of equilateral triangles – on famous buildings, landmarks and people. Possible projects to include The Empire State Building, The Amazon River, Bonny Langford, The Alhambra Palace in Granada, The Alhambra Palace Bingo & Social Club in Salford, The Great Pyramids, Dale Winton and anyone else who was in the cast of *Father Dear Father.*

19 Continue your Nobel prize-winning research to find a cure for Dengi Fever, The Common Cold, Tourettes Syndrome and the squits. Be careful to wash hands afterwards as the smell often offends.

20 Make a nice cup of tea, have a quick argument with that bone-head on reception, have a glance at the TV page of the newspaper and try to think of something nice to say about Robert Plant and Jimmy Page's solo careers. This is really, really hard, if not to say impossible. ·

# THE RUSS & JONO BREAKFAST EXPERIENCE GUIDE FOR Party VIRGINS

**Do you fail at parties? Do you spend more time in the kitchen talking to a bowl of twiglets than you do fumbling in the dark with a stranger's underwear? If so, these tried-and-tested tips will be your one-way ticket to party paradise!**

**Girls!** **Copy them on to the inside of your panties! Then every time you make a trip to the bathroom, you can do some last-minute cramming!**

**Boys!** **Copy them along the length of your Old Fella! That way you can get a good firm grip on any tricky party etiquette, and if you meet someone you really like, your notes will be a lot easier to read.**

## Why am I here?

Hopefully, because you've been invited. If not – don't panic. Simply assume 'crash' posture and bluff your way in.

Host: Er. Hello. Can I help you?
You: MY GOD! You haven't changed a bit! What is it? Ten . . . twelve years?* Oh . . . look, isn't that Joanna in there? I bet she won't recognise me. I used to be SO FAT, do you remember? Anyway, shall I put the beer in the fridge?

*(\* Not so good if you're crashing a ninth-birthday party.)*

**LOOKING COOL**

## Do I look good?

Unless your name is Swampy and you live in a mud tunnel somewhere under Salisbury plain, it's always a good idea to bathe before leaving home. Arriving with your arms full of towels and expensive French toiletries often makes for a clumsy party entrance – especially if you're about to assume the 'crash' posture. Ensure you know the dress code. At most parties it's 7739, though you do have three attempts to get it right.

## What time shall I turn up?

Try to get the timing right. Too early and you'll be mistaken for the caterer. Too late and they'll think you're a mini-cab driver.* Think about taking a gift. Since it's the thought that counts, this is a lot cheaper than actually buying something. Make sure your entrance is dramatic, entertaining and energetic (nothing quite beats skydiving on to the front lawn from a low flying Lancaster bomber).

*(\* Make sure you take your map book. At least you can make some money out of it.)*

## What about my coat?

If the weather is inclement, get your coat extremely wet and muddy before you get there. That way, on arrival you can rush upstairs and throw it on your host's best white bed linen along with the other hundred or so steaming, damp donkey jackets and cheap Aberdeen macs. If you're going to wear furs, make sure they're dead first.

Dazed and hungry ferrets scurrying up trouser legs in a dark room full of prancing drunks is a sure-fire recipe for disaster.

## I have a friend who wears a wig

Tell them to fasten it down properly. The onset of 'Hi-Ho-Silver Lining' or anything by The Pogues could herald a moment of deep public humiliation for you . . . er . . . or rather your friend.

## Shall I eat the food?

Remember they're pronounced 'croo-di-tays', and not 'crude-titties'. Avoid prawn cocktail vol-au-vents at all costs. They became illegal in 1992 and so, if you see any, they've probably been lying around in a cupboard since then. Buffets can be fun, but move away from the table at least once so other people can have a go. Guests like to take the weight off their feet when eating, so if you feel like breaking wind, don't do it standing next to a seated diner whose face is six inches from your arse. This is widely regarded as impolite.

## What about meeting people?

Meeting people can be a hazardous business, even for the hardened party-goer. Always keep on the move. If you look like you're constantly rushing to another part of the party, you won't get pinned down by the accountant from Cardiff who wants to tell you about his *Red Dwarf* video collection. But if you happen to bump into a drunk and mischievously-minded sex maniac who fancies the pants off you, you can conveniently forget why you were in a such a hurry. Never take your business cards to a party. You'll get wasted and hand them out to people who – if you were sober – you'd avoid like an open sewer. Don't spend any more time than you have to talking to losers. You needn't feel guilty about walking away from them 15 seconds into a conversation. A true loser will be used to it and will not take it personally.

## How do I spot the losers?

Losers come in many shapes and sizes. Easy to spot are the ones who sit on their own in the corner facing the wall while people stub cigarettes out on their head. Less obvious, but no less dangerous, are the ones who take over the stereo because they once did the disco at their brother-in-law's 21st birthday and so fancy themselves as a bit of a DJ.* Regardless of the exact nature of the loser's personality by-pass, THESE PEOPLE ARE HAZARDOUS and should be avoided at all costs. If a loser fixates on you, make your way to the bathroom, lock the door then climb out the window and re-enter the party downstairs. This will leave the loser standing on the upstairs landing for at least two hours, wondering why you're spending so long in the lavatory. This will then give you plenty of time to hang out with winners.

(*Which, coincidentally, is exactly how we began our illustrious careers.)

## And winners?

Be sure to hang out with winners, and not Winners. Short, irritating, talentless film directors are not pleasant company, unless you like running around a huge house in Holland Park with a pair of enormous Y-fronts on your head. Genuine winners can be found at the bar, telling hugely funny jokes and exuding charisma. Adopt all the outward signs of a winner by handing out drinks and cigarettes with care-free abandon. Make sure they're not your cigarettes, but the ones you nicked off the real winner when they went to the toilet.

## What about chat-up lines?

The only lines truly guaranteed to make you lots of friends at a party are the powdery white ones laid out on a bathroom mirror.* If this isn't an option, try some old favourites like 'Get your coat, you've just pulled', 'How do you like your eggs done in the morning?' or our personal favourite, 'We're famous DJs. Do you want to cop-off in the back of our Roller?'

(* Try reading Don't Get Sniffy With Me by Paul Merson and Frank Bough).

## Any chance of some sex?

By the time you've picked up the courage to proposition sex with someone you've only known for about 20 minutes, your alcohol-soaked brain will be running life support systems only. Once cerebral shut-down occurs, you're in deep trouble. Therefore the key to successful party sex is in memorising two simple rules for your prospective shag. The object of your desire should:

1. Walk on two legs
2. Be breathing

Stick to this, and you won't go far wrong.

## When should I leave?

Like your arrival, timing is crucial. Leave too early and you miss the high entertainment value of Cousin Frank disgracing himself in the garden. Too late, and you'll be there an extra three hours filling bin bags with empty cans, fag butts and half-finished bottles of Martini. Continue your clever impersonation of a winner by offering to pay for everyone's cab home and then booking a fleet of taxis using a former employer's account and password (oh, how rarely they change those codes . . . !).

Above all, be yourself! Unless of course you're a loser, in which case your best bet is to be somebody else.

# SO YOU WANNA BE A DJ RADIO PRESENTER?

Let's face it. There's never been a better time to be a DJ Radio Presenter than now. Hardly a day goes by without some new radio station springing up or some old has-been on Jurassic FM jumping before he's pushed and going on to sign on or face new challenges. Still, for all this new glasnost, radio is a cut-throat business that's harder to get into to than Brook Shields' knickers.

All the more reason then to find out if you, yes YOU, have what it takes to make it and go on to a life of untold wealth, fame, adulation and pally chats with the likes of Lynn Parsons, Kenny Everett (RIP), Ken Bruce, Simon Bates. Well this is the quiz that will tell you!

**PLEASE FILL QUIZ IN USING THE PEN
WITH DARKEST INK YOU CAN FIND.
SO IF YOU WANT TO DO IT TWICE
YOU'LL NEED TO BUY A NEW BOOK.**
                    **(Merciless bastard ED)**

## GENERAL RADIO KNOWLEDGE

**1)** Which of these two best encapsulates what you understand by the phrase 'a good old fashioned tranny'?

**2)** Which way up would you put this? (Please draw)

please draw answer here

That's absolutely disgusting. Try again using ink or lead pencil.

**3)** Which of these two buildings is NOT a centre of broadcasting excellence?
a) The leaning one.
b) BBC Broadcasting House.
c) Both.

## YOUR FELLOW PROFESSIONALS

**4)** Which one of the above could you work with?
a) All of them.
b) None of them.
c) Whoever of the above DOESN'T know Tony Blackburn.

**5)** Who is this?
a) Pat Sharp – radio and TV presenter, personality and all-round good egg.
b) Leif Garret – singer and failed candidate for 1972's 'Britain's Answer To David Cassidy'.
c) A big Girl's Blouse with silly, silly hair.

**6)** Study this picture carefully and answer the questions below.
a) Who is this man?
b) Why is this man still working?
c) How in the name of God above did he get away with it for so long?

**7)** Which of these Jimmie's would you feel most comfortable having as a baby sitter? Write an essay on the intuitions that have led you to make your choice.

## TECHNICAL KNOWLEDGE

**8)** What is this?
a) A compact disk used for producing crackle-free hi-fi sound.
b) A new kind of thin-crust pizza.
c) One of Kate Moss's breast implants.

**9)** What is a jingle?
a) A prerecorded piece of music used in radio programming as a bridging or transitional device.
b) Something bells do if your name's Santa Claus.
c) Where a dyslexic would go to try to find Tarzan.

**10)** What is a throw?
a) A smooth link or introduction to a prerecorded item or live studio pieces.
b) A nice patterned piece of material used to freshen that tired old chair or sofa.
c) What your mate Tony always does when he's had fourteen pints and a dodgy kebab.

## ABOUT YOU

**11)** Why do you want to be a DJ?
(On a scale of one to six)
a) Money                    1 2 3 4 5 6
b) Career satisfaction      1 2 3 4 5 6
c) Love of music          1 2 3 4 5 6
d) Undying love and respect for Richard Branson
              10 11 12 13 14 15 100

e) Because you were abused
   as a child and want to gain
   your vengeance on as
   many people as possible
                 1 2 3 4 5 6 7 8 88000
f) You get lots of free T-shirts and
   invitations to the kind of showbiz
   parties even Gary Bushell wouldn't go to.

**12)** As a person* would you say you are:
(Please tick)

- [ ] Sincere
- [ ] Flippant
- [ ] Caustic
- [ ] Childish
- [ ] Sentimental
- [ ] Mean-minded
- [ ] Pig-ignorant
- [ ] Monomaniacal (look it up)
- [ ] Greedy
- [ ] Lazy
- [ ] Hated By Most Of Your Friends
- [ ] Sexually frustrated
- [ ] A bit of a git

CANDIDATES ARE ADVISED THAT
ANYONE FAILING TO TICK LESS THAN
NINE OUT OF THE TEN ARE DEFINITELY
WASTING THEIR TIME.
* Not obligatory

**13)** You see a famous pop person across the
room at a terrible showbiz party. Do you:
a) Run over, shake their hand and start an
   interesting conversation about them?
b) Run over, shake their hand and start an
   interesting conversation about you?
c) Go to the bathroom and snort lots of
   Colombian marching powder with
   someone you really, really hate?

**14)** Meatloaf's 'Bat Out Of Hell' is
thirteen and a half minutes long. While this
is playing on the radio, do you:*
a) Nip out and have a dump?
b) Phone your agent and hassle for more
   gigs?

c) Schmooze the Programme Controller?
d) Get another six free Blur tickets off some
   girl you know at EMI?
e) Reprogramme the computer to crash
   during the busiest and most popular bit
   of your nearest ratings rival's show?
g) Deal in some penny shares and start
   your own business?
h) Call Australia to find out what the
   weather's like and if the azaleas have
   come out in the garden?
i) Scratch your arse and try to let off a big
   one without Trev your Producer noticing?

**15)** You hear rumours that the station is
about to drop you in favour of a younger,
hipper presenter. Do you:
a) Go gracefully and move on to a new,
   perhaps more suitable job with your
   listeners convinced you're doing so out
   of choice?
b) Become bitter and twisted and resign
   on-air in a fit of pique?
c) Erm . . . there really doesn't seem to be
   any other choice.

Congratulations!!
You are on the way to being a DJ. Now it's
time to actually apply for a job. Find a large
brown envelope, put a stamp on it, insert
your form and address it to:
> Matthew Bannister
> Head of String, Radio I FM
> BBC Broadcasting House
> Portand Place
> London W1

Don't forget to enclose a brief note about
exactly which drinking games you would
want to play after a particularly
dismal Road Show in Skegness.

   Good luck!!! And please remember
you don't have an absolute right to be a
DJ but you should always behave as
though you have.

*R & J Disclaimer: Absolutely none of these
options are, IN ANY WAY, at all based on our
own real-life activities but merely whimsical
fanciful notions being used solely for entertainment purposes.*

# DUMB

A terrified burglar decided to hide in a wardrobe when he heard an approaching police siren only to find that the house's owners were already in there – having kinky sex. When he was later arrested the horrified burglar told police that he would never try to rob David Mellor's place again. The case continues ... every week in the *News of the World*.

A bungling burglar called Louis Gomez used his mother's dress-making scissors to cut out the mask he wore for a bank raid in Valencia, Spain. Unfortunately for Señor Gomez the resulting holes were so big that he was totally recognisable and was picked out of an identity parade by six different witnesses the very next day. As they say in Spain *c'est la vie* ... that's the way the sangria crumbles.

A patient criminal with a literary streak was arrested for stealing over a hundred books from his local library – a page at a time. Working over a period of three years the word-hungry thief sliced each page out with a razor blade and hid it in the band inside his hat. When the court heard that the books in question were translations of the novels of a certain G. Archer, however, they decided the criminal had been punished enough and sentence was suspended pending psychiatric reports.

# CRIMES

A gang of inept robbers decided to blast their way into a cash-filled security van using high-powered blow torches. Fine. The van opened up like the Leicester City defence. Only trouble was that their unsubtle tool work had inadvertently led to the incineration of the entire contents of the safe – a hot ash-pile that worked out to be worth a cool £1.8 million. Nice one guys. Stick to hacksaws and sawn-off shotguns next time.

A blind man's hopes of pulling off the world's first politically-correct bank job were dashed when his disabilities turned out be a bit more, well, disabling than he had hoped. Five minutes after crashing through the doors of the *Banque de Paris* in Dax with his guidedog Belle, M. Jordan still had his pistol pointed at a large cactus. Unable to locate the staff he began to shout and issue threats to the wall. Eventually, when they had recovered from their laughter, security guards simply walked over to *Monsieur* Jordan, took the gun off him and arrested him. An FA spokesman denied that the Frenchman was serving out some of his sentence running around Premier League football grounds with a whistle in his hand and a baguette up his bum.

# The woman who predicted Russ and Jono's incredible rise to fame

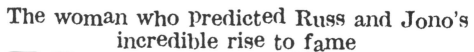

# Mystic Smeg

They first met her early in their broadcasting careers when Russ and Jono stopped by their London club for lunch. They'd seen snake acts from the exotic dancers there before, of course, but this one was different. Maybe it was the crud encrusted wellington boots, the fact that no one could work out where the snake had gone or simply the sight of her seventeen-stone frame gyrating across the stage that first caught their attention, but she was to have a profound influence on their lives from that moment on.

Joining them at their table, Mystic Smeg immediately predicted that her first pint would not touch the sides and downed

it in one. This was enough to convince the boys of her incredible powers and she has been guiding their careers ever since. Here Ms Smeg describes how you, too, can develop your own psychic powers . . .

'Make no mistake, using your powers isn't easy and, unless you're a Sagittarian fish-pond salesman who is wearing green and becoming sexually excited over someone whose name begins with J, it's going to be hard psychic work all the way. If you're ready, we can begin.

'Before I can even think about making my incredible predictions, I have to go through a secret ritual to open my channels, tune in to the psychic voices and make

sure that I don't get any interference from O'Reilly's Mini-Cabs down the road.

'There are a number of Ancient Ways of doing this, most of which involve tantric practices with farm animals that, thanks to numerous EEC directives and the vigilance of the RSPCA, are now a bit harder to pull off.

'My own method is simple. I go up to my special pink bathroom, lock the door, sit on the side of the bath and drink my mystical psychic potion which consists of three bottles of non-soporific Benylin washed down with a quart of unpasteurised turkey spunk and a case of Carlsberg Special Brew.

'Ten minutes later and for some magical reason, I find myself breaking through the plasma seal of this world into the other side. I am now receiving more messages that the Telecom Tower – and the charges are much more reasonable, too.

'The important thing to remember at this stage is to write each psychic message down as you make it up, otherwise you'll only have to start again afterwards and that can get a bit costly with the price of Special Brew these days.

'And that's all the secrets I'm prepared to reveal for this kind of money. Anybody got a fag?'

# Mystic Smeg's
## Top Ten Predictions

**1.** Killer dolphins will rise from the waves to terrorise tourists in the bazaars of Saudi Arabia and claim their rightful inheritance thus leading, for Taureans, to World War III.

**2.** Semolina will become the staple diet of the entire planet after Italy's surprise win in the last minute of extra time in the 1998 World Cup Final.

**3.** A Mr Whippy van will be discovered on the dark side of the moon. Though it will have run out of Flakes for the 99s, Librans looking for Witches' Hats or cider lollies will not go home disappointed.

**4.** An ancient dinosaur will be discovered alive and well in a large, three-storey house just off the King's Road in Chelsea, but those born under the sign of Cancer need not worry. Bill Wyman will be allowed to stay where he is and will not be taken off to the Natural History Museum.

**5.** The Nolan sisters will re-form and sweep to victory as the Upper Volta's entry in the 1998 World Eurovision Song Contest. The event will be married by a nasty incident when the Serbs take exception to the vote Taiwan have given to Peru and shell the jury.

**6.** American TV star Pamela Anderson will retire from show business to complete her PhD in Romance Languages and spend more time with her goldfish. Before leaving, she will donate her breasts to France to be turned into a new ski resort.

**7.** Pensioners will be able to get around properly when jet-propelled zimmer frames replace free bus passes. OAPs born under the sign of Pisces should go for the one with five-speed gears and imitation zebra-skin hand grips.

**8.** Les Dennis will attend a conference of ITV executives and reveal himself as the New Messiah come to tune us all into his truth vibrations. The executives will immediately sign him to go head to head over fifteen rounds with David Icke, who will eventually win a closely fought contest on the grounds that he has the more ridiculous hairstyle.

**9.** Observant and obsessive Capricorns who live in house number ten, have ten children, travel to work on the number ten bus, have ten fingers and toes or own a ten pound note will be involved in mass suicides all over the country when they drive themselves demented trying to work out what mystic significance there is in the fact that this Top Ten ends at number nine.

# CURRICULUM VITAE

# *Jonathan Coleman*

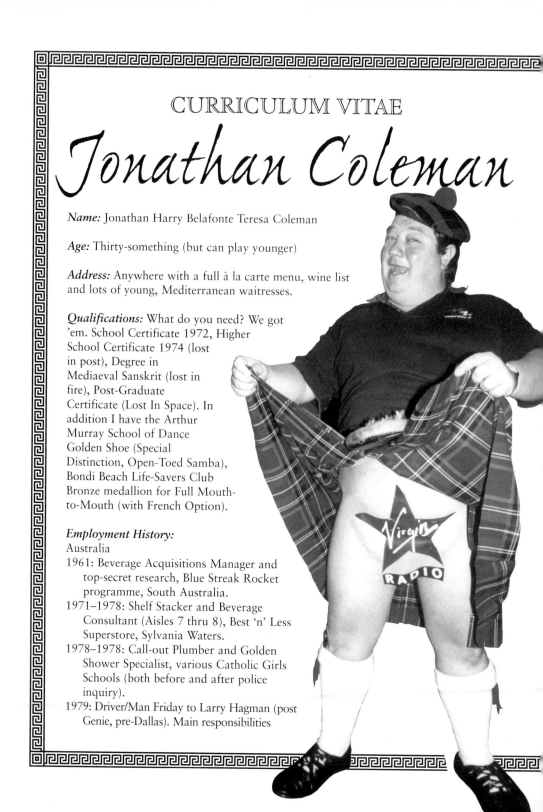

**Name:** Jonathan Harry Belafonte Teresa Coleman

**Age:** Thirty-something (but can play younger)

**Address:** Anywhere with a full à la carte menu, wine list and lots of young, Mediterranean waitresses.

**Qualifications:** What do you need? We got 'em. School Certificate 1972, Higher School Certificate 1974 (lost in post), Degree in Mediaeval Sanskrit (lost in fire), Post-Graduate Certificate (Lost In Space). In addition I have the Arthur Murray School of Dance Golden Shoe (Special Distinction, Open-Toed Samba), Bondi Beach Life-Savers Club Bronze medallion for Full Mouth-to-Mouth (with French Option).

**Employment History:**
Australia
1961: Beverage Acquisitions Manager and top-secret research, Blue Streak Rocket programme, South Australia.
1971–1978: Shelf Stacker and Beverage Consultant (Aisles 7 thru 8), Best 'n' Less Superstore, Sylvania Waters.
1978–1978: Call-out Plumber and Golden Shower Specialist, various Catholic Girls Schools (both before and after police inquiry).
1979: Driver/Man Friday to Larry Hagman (post Genie, pre-Dallas). Main responsibilities

included fielding calls from Betty Ford and solving his Rubic's Cube (without him knowing).

1979–1989: Failed Thriller Writer and persecuted Scout Master. Some charges still outstanding in the Isle Of Man and in Brunei but still hoping to get off with a good flogging.

1989: Left answer-phone message for Kurt Waldheim.

1990: Transported back to UK to answer charges of appearing on *Humdingers* and *TV-AM*.

Present: I find a book or a record token usually does the trick (as long as it's not over £5).

*Professional Appearances:*
*Acting:* King Lear in *King Lear*, Hamlet in *Hamlet* and Anne in *Anne Of Green Gables* (Charles Hawtrey Theatre, Eversley Junior School, Southgate)

I also played third hand from the left (ungloved) when the Black Theatre Of Prague visited the Black Hole Of Calcutta during a total eclipse which is why I've never had the critical acclaim I deserved for my work.

*Film:* Agfa-Colour 400 ASA (for Slides).

I also played the part of Distant Shopper Walking Away (Arm only) in *Star Wars* (prod: George Lucas). I've also done quite a lot of work in the *Making Of* series of films for TV and played a variety of corpses (Large Man Beaten Unconscious, Large Man Floating Face Down in Thames, Large Man in Dodgy Slacks) for *Crimewatch UK*.

*Radio:* In the kitchen, on the shelf, above the kettle. The one in the car's been stolen. Next time I'm definitely going to get one of those one's that you take out and put in your handbag.

*Interests:* Apart from myself, Indian, Italian, Malaysian, Thai, French, Anglo-Pacific, Chinese, Japanese and Australian food. I also worry a lot about Global warming, the population explosion and the scandalous waste of Mother Earth's precious raw-materials by such things as pointless Personality Christmas books.

*Special Skills:* Good firm handshake, crisp business card deployment and non-political baby-snogging. I also have six languages including French and Microsoft™ Works, Sixty wpm typing, the ability to break wind in perfect concert pitch and a full range of social skills including degree-level schmoozing and beginner's modesty.

*Referees:*

BOUTROUS-BOUTROUS GALI     RUPERT MURDOCH
UN BUILDING                               MASTER OF THE UNIVERSE
NEW YORK                                  c/o CENTAURS BUSINESS PARK
NEW YORK                                  ISLEWORTH
USA                                          MIDDX, UK

# Trev the HIPPY

Trev the Hippy, Russ and Jono's infamously brain-blasted producer, is a legend in his own newsagents'. The man who single handedly encouraged Rizla to invent the Kingsize Paper, Trev has kindly agreed to an interview with Edward Scissonshands.

[Editor's note: We apologise for the incoherence of this interview. It has been transcribed word for word to allow you to interpret it freely. Personally, I'm buggered if I know what Trev's going on about]

**ES:** Hi Trev. Thanks for agreeing to this interview.

**TREV:** What interview?

**ES:** Er.. this interview.

**TREV:** Oh, right. Like the vampire, yeah. *(Sound of sucking air between teeth. Giggles)*

**ES:** Um . . . Trev. What's your earliest memory?

**TREV:** Oh man, that's like radically difficult. I guess . . . er . . . the alarm clock.

**ES:** No Trev. Not your earliest memory today. In your whole life.

**TREV:** *(Giggles)* Oh yeah. *(sound of rustling papers)* Woodstock, man.

**ES:** The sixties rock festival?

**TREV:** No, that little bird in the Snoopy cartoons. He can't fly, right. And when he does, like, he just sort of hovers. Ever been on a hovercraft? It's like floating on a cushion of air, only in a boat.

**ES:** Trev?

**TREV:** Oh right man, sorry. Peanuts.

**ES:** Peanuts?

**TREV:** The Snoopy cartoon. There's this bird called Woodstock, and like it's really funny cos he can't fly properly.

**ES:** For God's sake, Trev, will you concentrate?

**TREV:** Sorry, man. Can you pass my lump of dope?

**ES:** What, this? *(Pause. Sound of large rock landing on desk)*. Trevor . . . er . . . do you take drugs?

**TREV:** No way, man. I always pay for them.

**ES:** Right. You're a man who's heavily into . . .

**TREV:** . . . dope?

**ES:** . . . music. What's your favourite?

**TREV:** Er . . . Skunk.

**ES:** Anansie?

**TREV:** Er, no, Amsterdam I think.

**ES:** I'm talking about bands.

**TREV:** I know, man, fascist state or what? Banned from growing it, banned from smoking it, banned from eating it. Cake?

**ES:** Oh, that's very kind of you. *(Sound of munching.)* This has a very unusual flavour. What's in it?

**TREV:** Black

**ES:** Black what?

**TREV:** Just black, man. Just black.

**ES:** Oh . . . OK *(hic)*. Erm . . . er . . . Trev.

**TREV:** Yes, man *(Sound of a match being lit. Then puffing on large cigarette.)*

**ES:** I'm feeling a bit funny.

**TREV:** You look a bit funny *(Both giggling. Escalates into prolonged laughter. Uncontrollable snorting and guffawing. Sound of someone falling off their chair.)*

**ES:** Hey, Trev, now I'm the floor manager! *(Fifteen minutes of uncontrollable laughter. Eventually subsides into sniggers.)*

**TREV:** So, like, anymore questions?

**ES:** For what?

**TREV:** The interview, man.

**ES:** Oh yeah . . . Can I have another cake?

**TREV:** Munch, man, munch. Pot noodle?

**ES:** Oh YEAH! *(Sound of eating.)* When you first started your career, what drove you into radio?

**TREV:** My dad, in a 1964 Austin Cambridge.

**ES:**
**TREV:** } HA! HA! HA!

*(Tape becomes unintelligible from this point forward. Interview suspended.)*

## EDWARD & SHANKA'S BEST OF THE NEWS HEADLINES

**Cured ham . . . it's a miracle say Vatican doctors.**

Dentists are now warning that kissing can severely loosen your teeth – especially if your wife finds out about it.

Thank you very much indeed

**Car news now. The Lada car company is to recall this year's new model after it was discovered that the cardboard used in the fenders was dangerously sub-standard.**

Angus McSporran from Aberdeen won over £5 million on the National Lottery and celebrated with a lavish breakfast of champagne and porridge. When asked if he anticipated any problems with begging letters, he said, 'Not really. I'll just keep sending them.'

90% OF AMERICAN MEN SAY THEY'VE ONLY HAD ONE SEX PARTNER IN THE LAST 12 MONTHS – MADONNA.

Thank you very much indeed

The world's fattest man, fifty-five stone Jose Silva has died at his ranch in South America. In accordance with his final wishes he will be cremated today in Sao Paulo and his ashes scattered over Brazil . . . Chile, Paraguay, El Salvador and Bolivia.

Thank you very much indeed

SURVIVORS OF A PLANE CRASH IN THE ANDES ADMITTED TURNING TO CANNIBALISM TO SURVIVE. THEY DIDN'T REALLY HAVE A CHOICE. IT WAS EITHER THAT OR EAT THE AIRLINE FOOD.

MacDonald's have opened a fast-food restaurant in the holy town of Lourdes. Business has been brisk . . . especially since they put French Friars and Palm Sundaes on the menu.

A cinema in Penzance has been rocked by an explosion causing over 300 theatregoers to be evacuated. As one of them later said, 'If I'd wanted to see a bomb I'd have booked tickets to see *The Dale Winton Show*.'

Foreign news now. An eleven-year-old Australian boy has successfully sued his parents for naming him 'Fatso'. As the tearful little chap left the courtroom he paid tribute to the support he'd received during the week-long hearing from his two brothers Lardbutt and Wobblechops.

**Thank You Very Much Indeed.**

# THE RUSS & JONO BREAKFAST EXPERIENCE GUIDE FOR Literary VIRGINS

**AND BOY DO WE MEAN INSTANT.** This is your chance to become an author in a best-selling book RIGHT NOW. Forget all that tedious stuff about going on writers' courses or burning the midnight oil. All you have to do is pick up a pen or crayon or any sharp object, write what the hell you like in the space below and Hey Presto! You can go into your work or secure unit and impress everybody by telling them that you wrote a page in the best-selling book by Russ & Jono. It couldn't be simpler. Go on. Be our guest. Unleash the Salman Rushdie within you (so that's where he's hiding).

**There. That was fun wasn't it?** Now you can start that thirteen-part novel set in winter on the Russian Steppes as a family of Cossacks, embittered by the corruption of the Tsarist court, uproot themselves . . .

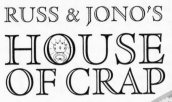

# RUSS'S ROUGH GUIDE TO
# ALIENS

**WARNING!!** The following page contains material that readers of a sensitive disposition may find deeply disturbing . . . especially if they've got a Lean Cuisine Beef Stew Meal For One strapped to their lower abdomen.

Here are a list of common questions I'm often asked by complete strangers about my top-secret Alien research. Naturally names and places have been changed to protect the ignorant.

Brian Laudrup of Glasgow asks . . .
What do Aliens look like?

Well, Brian. Contrary to popular myth, Aliens do not look like a cross between Norman Lamont and Andrew Lloyd Webber. I've found most of them are even uglier than that. In short there are three distinct races of Alien life forms.

THE GREYS: These have large beards, large almond-shaped eyes, large bodies with grey rhinolike skin and incredibly large penises (except in Scotland where the weather has its usual effect). Greys can also be very tall – usually around about three or four hundred feet. (This can be useful to know if you're ever called upon to put together an inter-gallatic basketball team.)

THE GREENS: These are an extremely boring species with appalling dress sense and dodgy, slightly garlicy breath. Sitings are rare though Andi Peters and Emma Forbes seemed to have the knack of getting one to appear every week on *Live & Kicking*.

Ironically, the emissions from the Green's space ships are almost certainly responsible for the hole in the ozone layer. This fact is being kept back from the public by a conspiracy between the Greens and Ken Dodd's Secret World Government (see section on Black Budgets on the internet @tax return.what's that diddy?

THE VAGUES: These are undoubtedly the most malevolent and dangerous of all the 567 types of Alien species identified by the Pontypridd Centre For Extra-Terrestial Research. Their activities include well-poisoning, child-snatching, putting needless cones down on the junction between the M1 and M6 just after Spaghetti junction and forcing Terry Wogan at laser point to carry on presenting *Children In Need*. One less sinister side to this extraordinary Alien race is their willingness to share technology with mankind. They were for instance directly responsible not only for the fax machine and the compact disc but for being the only Alien race prepared to tell mankind how to open milk cartons without spilling the contents down your trousers.

Betty Boo of Newcastle-Upon-Tyne asks . . . Why are they coming here?

Well, Ms Boo. This rather depends on which race you're talking about. The Greys, for instance are a very leisure-orientated race and after a hard millennium at work like to enjoy weekends that last up to twenty thousand years. A visit to Earth to the Greys is the equivalent of a weekend mini-break to Amsterdam – with free tulips thrown in.

The Greens have our best interest at heart. Their aim is to rid the world of all that is evil and destructive. Theyir most recent projects include nuclear, famine, drug abuse and

getting *Lucky Ladders* knocked off the ITV schedule for good.

The Vagues are only here for the beer and the young German boys.

Curly Watts of Eaton Square, London asks . . . Will they ever go away?

Good question, Curly. The short answer is no, not unless we take *Coronation Street* off the air. Like 15 million Brits all Alien species just can't get enough of soaps. The Greys have even named one of their 345 moons after Ena Sharples and there's a street in Zeta Reticuli called Albert Tatlock Crescent. Two years ago the BBC made a desperate attempt, at the direct request of Ken Dodd's Secret Government to rid us of the Alien Menace when they broadcast over a hundred episodes of *Elderado*. Unfortunately this backfired when the Aliens discovered they rather liked it and when the series ended they abducted Pilar and installed her on the other planet she's been on all along. I would like to point out that intergalactic relations during this time were extremely strained.

Barbara Windsor of Windsor asks . . . Are we in danger?

Yes.

Chris Evans of Pitlochry asks . . . What is their culture like?

Well, Chris. In general terms all the cultures are quite similar. Imagine a cross between the Ottoman Empire and Butlin's Selsey Bill and you won't go far wrong. Of course, the Vagues don't have the Knobbly Knees competition but they're very big on the egg-and-spoon race.

But there are differences. When it comes to sport The Greys embrace what they call The Gazza Way. It's quite common in the Grey Premier League to see teams going out on the field after 17 pints of lager, ten Mars Bars and a steaming-hot vindaloo curry and chucking up on the penalty spot. The Greens don't play sport unless they've got the written permission of each blade of grass first.

Jimmy Saville of Christ College, Cambridge asks . . . What should I say to an Alien if approached?

Well, Jimmy. Don't try jangle-jangle-jewellry-jewellery. Material possesions, especially those proferred by dodgy old men in big leather armchairs are of no interest to them.

This is the form of wording agreed at the last Pontypridd International Alien Conference. 'Is that a laser-beam molecular de-stabiliser in your pocket or are you just another friend of Lindford Christie's.'

When it comes to the Grey's BEWARE!! They are completely telepathic apart from a few of the newer arrivals who are still waiting for BT to come round and plug them in.

# ALIEN PHENOMENA

The following photos are exclusive extracts from my own personal, top-secret UFO archive [ED: A £1.99 Boots photo album hidden in an old shoe-box under the bed.}

A GREYS' CRAFT

0543207900?  POLAROID

A GREENS' CRAFT

THE VAGUES' CRAFT

Alien animal mutilations are on the increase. Sadly last year my very own dog, Lucky, fell victim to one such attack.

One of the most worrying Alien-related phenomena is abduction. This has happened to me many times, strangely enough when I'm on my way to visit my local council tax office. Here is a disturbing photo my Mum took during my thirteenth abduction experience.

*Although the information contained on these pages is deeply disturbing, please remember the likelihood of you being taken roughly from behind by one of the Vagues is, unfortunately, extremely rare.*

*Sleep well.*

Coming soon on a page near you: Russ William's reveals the truth behind Eric Von Daniken's bizarre Inca marriage to Anna Ford with the Loch Ness monster as best man.

# THE RUSS & JONO BREAKFAST EXPERIENCE GUIDE FOR Lottery VIRGINS

Hey there! Don't be downhearted just because you haven't won the lottery yet. When it comes to picking those winning numbers you need a high level of skill and supreme confidence. Since you probably have all the numeracy skills of Ken Dodd's tax accountant and as much self-esteem as a baked bean, you've absolutely no chance.

But don't worry, help is at hand in the form of Russ & Jono's high-tech, state-of-the-art number rota system similar to the one used by many former Tory cabinet ministers and all of the world's millionaire industrialists. This system is so highly thought of by high rollers that it is kept in a huge Swiss bank vault and only ever glanced at by us when we visit our own personal Gnome of Zurich when we're running a bit low on the old 'fun vouchers'.

So sit back and get ready to strike it rich – the Russ and Jono way. Above all don't lose confidence, and keep on trying. Remember that a wise man once said that if you put a hundred monkeys in a room with a hundred typewriters for a hundred years, eventually they would run out of bananas.

Simply choose one of these easy-to-use selection grids, but please keep it to yourself. Never photocopy this winning system or discuss it with any members of the legal profession as they are all crooks.

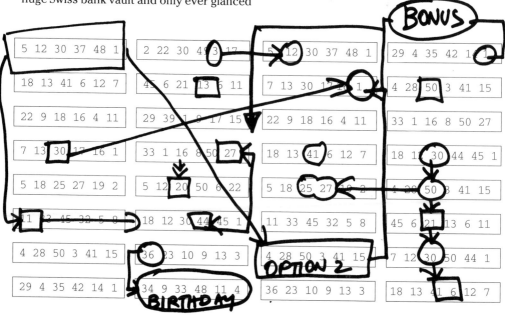

# RUSS & JONO'S
# HOUSE OF CRAP
## PRESENT

**NEW!**

## FROM THE
# PINEAPPLE
### NETWORK

### THE NETWORK WITH THE
# *Heavenly*
#### TOUCH

Hey! Yes you? Aren't you just sick of all those ads for mobile phones that seem like they're going to help you choose which phone and which network you're going to sign up for and only end up confusing you even more? Yes. Good. Then we've got the phone for YOU!

Forget all this confusing talk of analogue and digital, personal tariffs and business tariffs. Why don't you just get on line with one of these superb solid state Indonesian mobile phones. Built by some of Jarkata's finest child-slave labour using nearly all new parts they represent not only a huge technological leap backward but excellent value for money too. Just look at the features on this baby.

 Hands Free – ideal for Saudi-Arabian shoplifters who just have to stay in touch.

 Crackle Free CD quality sound. CD's include Tammy Winnett and Bryan Adams !! (Does not apply when unit is operative).

 Voice-Male. Featured voices include Robert Maxwell, George Benson and Phyllis from Coronation Street.

 Special Weekend Low Rates. If you're feeling depressed or suicidal o a Saturday and Sunday we'll pe you up by doubling our charges that'll give you something else to worry about !!

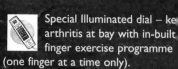 Special Illuminated dial – ke arthritis at bay with in-built finger exercise programme (one finger at a time only).

 Special Low-Cal Long Batte Life. Special 12 volt battery gives you a mammoth 8 ho talk time (minimum call). Can aid weight loss only if used in conjunctio with calorie-controlled diet or carrie around for more than ten yards.

 New Improved Aerial – now 20% longer and 40% more effective with mixed colours at low temperatures.

Place your order NOW! by calling us on your mobile NOW! on a special order line number 1-800-Sucka. (No timewasters please). REMEMBER for every five Pineapple phones ordered we'll send you one free imitation leather carrying case absolutely FREE (Does not include case)

NB. Pineapple Mobiles cannot be used in the UK.

Have you had it with the National Lottery? Are you sick of waiting in every Saturday night in the hope of megabucks only to find that all you get is one number and another drubbing at the hands of sickly-sweet Anthea? You are? Well at last you really have the chance to win and WIN BIG with Russ & Jono's Spot The Ball.

# SP⬤T THE BALL

**WIN £150 000 CASH ON THE SPOT !!**

*Don't forget to close the ball before we go to print. Cheers mate — Russ*

MATCH: Dour 0-0 draw between Arsenal Reserves & Staines 1st Team
CONDITIONS: Shitty
DATE: God knows.
GROUND: Wormwood Scrubs

**All you have to do to win BIG MONEY is pin point the exact position of the centre of the ball. Take note of the conditions, the teams and the gradient of the pitch and use your skill and judgment to WIN.**

RUNNERS UP PRIZES INCLUDE:
A tour round the Manchester City Trophy room to see their lovely blue carpet
AND
A night out with Paul Merson in Colombia.

SEND YOUR COUPON TO:
SPOT THE BALL COMPETITION
c/o Adolf Hitler Unit
Sky Television
South Australia (just up from the Rundle Mall)
Britain

Please note: Entrants must be over 87 years old and have their coupons counter-signed by both parents)

**Good luck.
GET SPOTTING !!!**

# Sad but True

Aussie driver Andy Smedley came to a horribly sticky end after blowing such a large bubble with his favourite brand of chewing gum that he couldn't see where he was going. His car swerved off the road, crashed through a protective barrier and plunged over a 300ft cliff into the shark-infested sea below. Sad to see yet another great blowjob going to waste.

Lucky, an eight-year-old pet Alsatian dog, saw his doggy life go up in smoke when he cocked his leg as usual against a lamppost outside his house and was electrocuted by a 240-volt shock. Poor Lucky's owner was also injured when he went to stroke his now frazzled ex-man's best friend. As he said later to police, 'It was terrible.'

Thrifty Italian mourners were treated to a surpise Two-For-The-Price-Of-One spectacular recently in Palermo when an eighty-three-year-old woman was so overcome with grief at the death of her husband that she dropped down dead when he being buried – and toppled into the grave beside him. Reports that the Government has been considering borrowing the idea to save on funeral expenses for the old and the unemployed here in Britain have been vehemently denied.

Who says gardening isn't a blood sport? Not Mrs Eileen Campbell from the West Midlands anyway, after her 68 year-old husband Dick toppled off his ladder while trimming a tree in their back garden and cut his head off with his strimmer. Still, as Mrs Campbell later said, it wasn't all that bad. Dick died while applying the finishing touches to the job so at least she won't have to do the job herself until next year.

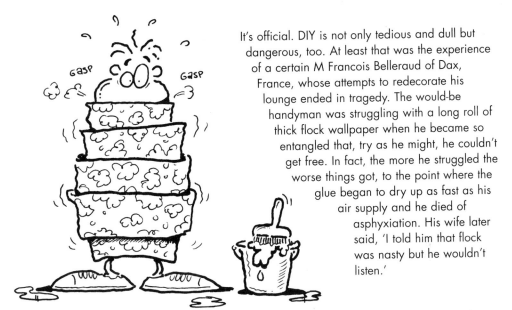

It's official. DIY is not only tedious and dull but dangerous, too. At least that was the experience of a certain M Francois Belleraud of Dax, France, whose attempts to redecorate his lounge ended in tragedy. The would-be handyman was struggling with a long roll of thick flock wallpaper when he became so entangled that, try as he might, he couldn't get free. In fact, the more he struggled the worse things got, to the point where the glue began to dry up as fast as his air supply and he died of asphyxiation. His wife later said, 'I told him that flock was nasty but he wouldn't listen.'

The fine art of train-surfing has long been practised on the Indian subcontinent as thousands of non-paying passengers seek to avoid the inconvenience of crowded carriages and difficult ticket collectors by making their journey up on the roof. Unfortunately for six young lads making a trip from the country up to Delhi, this usually convenient arrangement went a bit awry when the train went under a newly-constructed bridge at 90 miles an hour killing them instantly. Ironically the six lads were only on the train because they were on their way to apply for new jobs – as ticket collectors on the very train on which they were killed.

Every year around the world dozens of people are hit by flying objects – mostly those thrown by Chelsea fans. None could be more unfortunate than a Brazilian gentleman named Antonio Valdar, however, who was innocently walking through the business district in Rio when a typewriter fell out of the sky and killed him. The machine, it later transpired, was thrown by a lawyer who had become so infuriated at the sloppiness of his secretary's typing that he had picked up her typewriter and thrown it at her. The secretary had obviously seen this coming and ducked, leaving the machine to fly out of the window and make it's ten-thirty appointment with the top of poor Mr Valdar's head. Who says lawyer's offices are dull places where nothing interesting ever happens?

Jonathan Coleman

The power of the animal rights lobby grows daily. Their most recent triumph was the cancellation of the annual steer-wrestling competition in Amarillo, Texas. As a shocked and outraged would-be steer wrestler said 'Them animal rights people are gettin' their asses in a spin over nothin', boy. All that happens is that three of us jump a 500 pound steer, wrestle it to the ground and slip a pair of silk ladies panties on it. Now what the hell is wrong with that?' Rumours that Opra Winfrey has offered to help the guys out instead proved to be just another post PC white-supremacist fantasy.

Hospital doctors really do take some diabolical liberties sometimes, don't they? Not content to merely wander around the wards looking smug and sexually satisfied in dodgy kipper ties, top American surgeon Edward Baker drew smiley faces on his male patients' penises. When finally disciplined for this strange, humiliating habit he claimed he only created his manhood masterpieces 'to relieve stress'. The rumour that both Julian Clary and Michael Portillo have rushed to book themselves into the same hospital with unspecified abdominal problems has been denied by a spokesman.

The Ukrainian national lottery, like that in Britain, is a huge success with more than two million tickets sold every week which is even more of a marketing coup because there are no cash prizes. Instead Ukrainian punters are offered a conveyor-belt of delights that includes such luxuries as rolls of toilet paper, toothpaste, soap, jars of beetroot and even cans of engine oil. The British tabloids confirmed today that they will not be trying to track down winners for publicity purposes.

UKRANIAN LOTTERY

BEETROOT

# Globe

American cops sure have it tough what with drive-by shootings and all those black motorists to beat up. Spare a thought though for one poor, unfortunate patrolman who was attacked in a place where no armour could protect him when his own dog went mad and bit his penis. The incident occurred when Jim Travis of Tucson, Arizona was about to make love to his wife with a slice of salami (don't ask) wrapped around his pride and joy. Obviously Mr and Mrs Travis weren't the only ones who found this an exciting break from domestic routine as their Dobermann pinscher Sammy leapt up and made his painful contribution to his owner's love life. The fact that a number of Tory MPs now own Dobermann pinschers is entirely coincidental.

Things are getting pretty crazy in Italy, especially in the court-rooms of Palermo, Sicily where a housewife is asking for £1.5 million in damages because her husband thinks that he's a duck. Anita Pugnohas told the court that her husband Giovanni became convinced he had joined the ranks of our feathered friends immediately after a crate fell on his head at work. The court was moved by her tearful account of life with someone who spends his days running around quacking, flapping his arms about and biting himself clean in the bath. When it came to judgment times, though, the jury was bitterly divided over what to do with Giovanni – with three going for the orange sauce, two for a simple casserole with pasta and red peppers and the rest opting to have Giovanni in a crispy Chinese style with pancakes. As for the man himself, he was too busy diving for pieces of bread in a local pond to comment.

Lots of Love
Russ Williams xxx
"UP THE SPURS!"

# LOST IN Showbiz

Kathleen Turner, who has played her fair share of loonies on stage and screen (remember her as the mother who bumped off anyone who annoyed her kids?), including the famous lush Tallulah Bankhead, has recently purchased a four-bedroom, 25th-floor-apartment in Manhattan. She obviously believes 'it's good to talk' because she's had no less than 12 telephone lines installed. Maybe she wants to make sure she won't be crossed out of Jack Nicholson's phone book.

Florida palm trees just weren't good enough for decorating the garden of Sylvester Stallone's £6 million Miami mansion. Oh, no. The arboreally-challenged Sly had to have £400,000 worth of Californian palms shipped in instead. Apparently, according to Sly, Florida palms are 'too short'. Sylvester Stallone is 5ft 10in tall.

The massive Italian opera singer Luciano Pavarotti was so worried about his weight that he put himself in prison. The ton-up tenor hired three special 'diet cops' to watch his every move and stop him sneaking out in the middle of the night and raiding the fridge. The plan was so successful – he lost 75 pounds – that Pavarotti has extended the scheme. In addition to his diet cops he now has classic cops, caffeine free cops and cherry cops, too.

Ageing romeo Jack Nicholson hired a secretary (shouldn't that be archeologist) to go through his personal phone book and, as Jack charmingly put it, 'scratch out all the dead people'. When the secretary asked how she was supposed to know who was alive and who wasn't her employer said. 'Just call 'em up and if they don't answer the phone they must be dead.'

# Celebrity

Delia Smith

Tim Burton

Charles Asnavour

Eddie Izzard

Suggs

# Gallery

Oiling up to the stars with Russell Grant

Ulrika

Harry Hill

Jackie Collins

Sarah-Jane and Baby Spice

# THE RUSS & JONO BREAKFAST EXPERIENCE GUIDE FOR
# Business
## VIRGINS

Nothing can beat the extraordinary sense of freedom you get when you're your own boss (with the possible exception of running stark naked across Salisbury Plain with the sun on your back and peanut butter in your hair. But..er.. we'll talk about that later) Running your own business is a joy shared by millions. It may be hard work now and again, but this is hugely compensated by the intoxicating power of seeing your bank balance choking to the brim with piles of stinking lucre, and the orgasmic joy of ordering your lackeys around like some half deranged megalomaniac Caligula.

For most people, the thought of starting a business is fraught with worry and danger – although the biggest stumbling block is peoples' unwillingness to get off their fat arses and actually give it a go. Let's

face it – right now all you have to do is drag yourself out of bed five or six times a week, stagger blearily into work, make a half-hearted attempt to keep the boss happy for a few hours, stumble home again, and in return you get enough money to keep you in beer and fags for the month.

But we happen to think our Breakfast Experience listeners are made of sterner stuff than this. You're people of vision. People with big ideas, people who shape the world. And you're all crooks – which makes you perfect for running a business.

## STARTING THE BUSINESS

Before you start your business, you should think about starting your business. In business-speak, the above heading was a 'product ahead of its time', so we're withdrawing it immediately.

## THINKING ABOUT STARTING YOUR BUSINESS

That's better. Thinking about starting your business is all about asking yourself lots of questions. Try playing Trivial Pursuit on your own, for instance, or watching 15-1 with that nice William G.Stewart man. Alternatively, you could act like a grown-up for thirty seconds and ask some proper questions.

## WHAT SORT OF BUSINESS SHOULD I START?

It doesn't matter. Some people get all hung up about their 'skills base', their 'qualifications' or their 'experience'. The only experience you need is the one you hear on your radio every morning, and even that's pushing it a bit. You just need guts, bollocks, a backbone, a steely jaw, a tight arse, brains, the heart for it, and something to sink you teeth into.

## HOW DO I IDENTIFY A MARKET?

They usually have trestle tables, plastic awnings and loads of crappy bootleg

Spice Girls T-shirts that disintegrate on the first wash. For business success, however, you need one thing. Stupid people with money to spend. And if you can get them to spend it on you, then you're laughing. I mean, you bought this book didn't you? Ha! Ha! Ha!

## BUT I DON'T KNOW WHAT TO SELL!

So what? Most people don't know what to buy. Make something up. How about Tiawanese Skin Cream made from Essence of Monkey Spunk? Donkey Cock Herbal Tea? The Vanessa Feltz Celebrity Enema and Pessary two-in-one kit? Whatever you make, someone's bound to want to buy it. And that's all down to marketing.

## WHAT'S MARKETING?

Lying. But it's a special type of lying done by tossers who drive 5-series BMWs, have mobile phone implanted on the side of their heads and always shout "Crispen darling, grab a

bottle of Bollie and come here" over the top of your head in pretentious London restaurants. Having said that, these people use words like 'demographics', 'market penetration', and 'brand equity' while keeping a straight face, and they manage to convince Joe Public to spend his hard earned cash on stuff he'll never, ever want or need.

## HOW DO I LAUNCH MY COMPANY?

Set it on a wooden ramp by the side of the river, get a major international celebrity such as Russ Williams or Jonathan Coleman (if you feel this is setting your sights too high then try a less popular celebrity such as Richard Branson or the Spice Girls) and have them smash a bottle of champagne on it. Celebrities, of course, charge a great deal of money for performing such services, but we are worth every penny.

## MANAGING YOUR BUSINESS

There's only two things that keep business going: stupid people with money (see above) and handshakes. In business, men and women are judged only by their handshake. Nobody buys from an entrepreneur who hasn't got a good handshake, and if you're useless at it, your business will suffer. For instance, if you've got a good hard, firm one, you're interests will just grow and grow and grow. Limp, soft and insipid, and you're bound to go belly up.

## SO WHAT MAKES THE PERFECT HANDSHAKE?

First, ensure you've got a hand. Caption Hook was renowned for his bad business acumen, and many put this down to the fact that every time he tried to shake hands on a deal, he cut off fingers, slashed arteries and generally made a real nuisance of himself.

As this picture shows, the perfect handshake is firm but fair, with hands that are freshly laundered, powered, manicured and belonging to the two greatest living DJs of their time. Obviously, you can't have our hands, since we use them quite a bit. This means your handshake will likely be crap, regardless of how much you practice.

This picture shows a truly terrible handshake. Obviously it will gain you instant access into any Freemasonry Organisation or church event run by the Knights of the Templar, but these days that counts for very little. In business this is a sure fire way of revealing your true identity as one of the Royal Family, or a member of British Intelligence – both of which will destine you to business oblivion.

## STAYING SUCCESSFUL

The key to staying successful in business is employing people who are smarter than you, work harder than you, and get paid an awful lot less than you. This allows you to 'empower' them (they'll never work out what that means) whilst you can spend more of your free time having sex with people who are after you for your money. But since you know they're after your money, it doesn't matter.

## WHAT IF MY BUSINESS FAILS

Your business will only fail if you lose a small amount of money. If you lose huge, disgustingly immoral and unfeasibly enormous amounts of money, the banks'll bail you out forever, and you can continue to lead the life to which you've become accustomed.

Get the debt high enough, and you'll qualifying as a third world nation in your own right and then you never have to give it back

# EDWARD & SHANKA'S

# BEST OF THE NEWS HEADLINES

Ex-cop John Stalker has been finally called in by worried officials to investigate Leicester City's 'Shoot To Miss' policy.

Thank you very much indeed

The world's newest cult religion held its first press conference today. The 'Holy Order Of The Frisbees' is a religion based on reincarnation. They believe that when you come back you either land on a garage roof or get taken away by a dog and hidden in a bush at the bottom of the garden.

Thank you very much indeed

Literary news. Barbara Cartland today publishes her 560th novel, thus keeping up her amazing record of producing one book for every year of her life.

Euro-Disney is to close, after the shock discovery of giant mouse in kitchen.

Thank you very much indeed

Top tycoon Richard Branson got himself into a pickle yesterday when he admitted that yes, he too had recently joined the mile-high club . . . strangely enough during a solo balloon flight over the Indian Ocean.

Cornish Police yesterday claimed to have recovered two kilos of cannabis with a street value of over a million pounds . . . which means that they must be paying much more for it than the rest of us.

Thank you very much indeed

COLIN STAGG IS TO SUE THE POLICE – STING, STUART AND ANDY ARE SAID TO BE IN A STATE OF SHOCK, SAYS THE BAND'S LAWYER.

Thank you very much indeed

**Britain's first dyslexic fetishist's convention in Birmington proved to be a major flop when a 40ft banner advertising the event was found to read 'Bondage fanatics of the world untie.'**

The Home Secretary signalled a new seriousness in his Get Tough On Crime policy when he announced a much harsher prison regime. In a bid to make prison a grimmer, tougher place that no one wants to go back to he's bringing in the guy who designs the interiors for Happy Eater restaurants.

**Thank You Very Much Indeed.**

# THE RUSS & JONO BREAKFAST EXPERIENCE GUIDE FOR
# ACTUAL VIRGINS

*Blokes! As far as your mates are concerned, you're a one man shag machine. Your pants are seeing more action than the whole of Warren Beatty's underwear draw during the filming of his famous action movie "30 Birds on My Face". Big girls, short girls, thin girls, fat girls. Let's face it, you're beating them off with a shitty stick.*

*Well.... That's what your mates think anyway. But we know different, don't we? In real life you couldn't get your leg over if you were the last man on Earth.*

*Until now!*

*Don't worry that you're intensely boring, ugly, smelly and slightly sinister. We can get you inside any pair of panties you like, with this Insti-Shag-Babe-Magnet-Mask(tm). Simply cut around the edges, fix to your face with a dab or two of Superglue, and Hey Presto! Clean your teeth and change your underwear – you've bought a First Class ticket to Copping Off Central.*

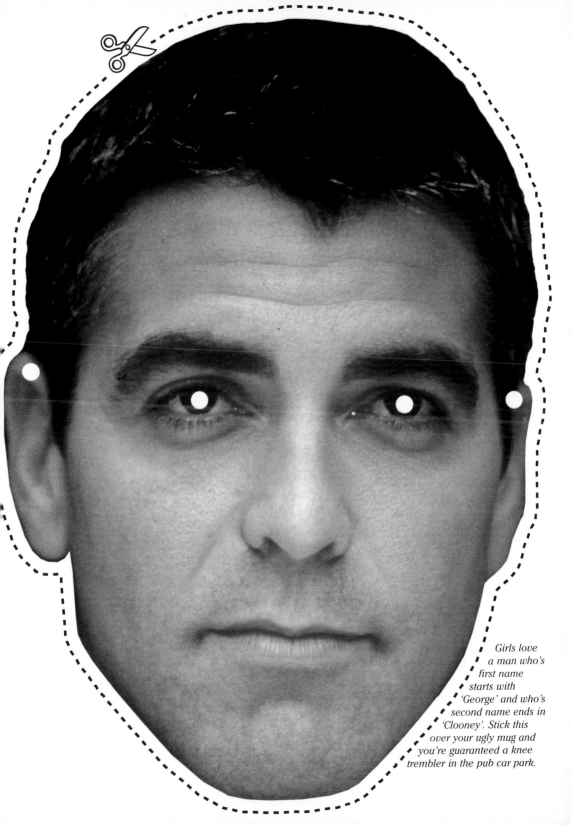

*Girls love a man who's first name starts with 'George' and who's second name ends in 'Clooney'. Stick this over your ugly mug and you're guaranteed a knee trembler in the pub car park.*

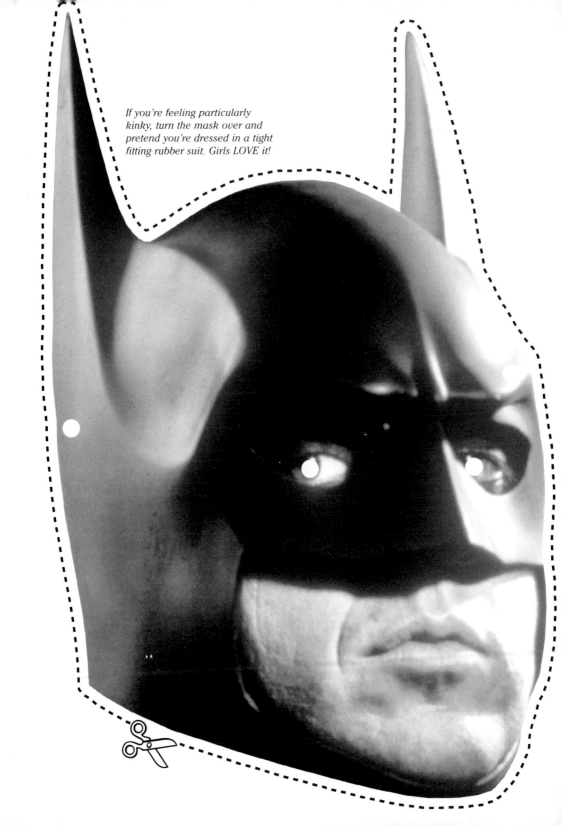

*If you're feeling particularly kinky, turn the mask over and pretend you're dressed in a tight fitting rubber suit. Girls LOVE it!*

# WORD-SEARCH PUZZLE THING

Just to squeeze an extra few minutes' entertainment from this fantastic book, we've made up one of those interesting word search puzzle things. Hidden in this grid are 30 words chosen randomly from the world of showbiz, DIY and quality pet-care. Simply find them, mark them with a pencil, and then cut out the page and send it to your own address. Everyone's a winner!

Dear *(write your own name here)*

_____

Congratulations! You're a winner in the Russ and Jono Breakfast Experience Back of the Book Quiz. Since our budgets were a bit low, we can't afford to send you a prize. However, we know that you mutilated our book in order to enter this competition, so we're returning this page to you so you can stick it back in and repair the damage.

Alternatively, you can frame this page as proof to all your mates that you won the competition. Well done!

| R | A | Y | L | L | E | J | Y | K | B | T | R | W | E | F |
|---|---|---|---|---|---|---|---|---|---|---|---|---|---|---|
| I | Y | O | U | R | W | I | F | E | S | A | S | L | U | T |
| C | C | H | I | P | O | M | Z | Q | D | M | P | U | B | E |
| H | D | S | W | P | G | M | J | I | H | P | U | B | R | V |
| A | N | D | R | E | A | Y | O | T | I | O | N | O | E | I |
| R | U | S | S | E | N | O | T | N | L | N | K | A | A | R |
| D | N | E | Z | C | N | O | Y | E | L | A | Y | R | K | G |
| A | I | D | X | E | P | M | O | I | I | P | M | D | F | I |
| N | C | Z | I | S | K | A | K | L | U | N | O | L | A | N |
| D | E | S | P | C | K | D | O | X | J | O | N | O | S | R |
| J | P | M | I | H | H | F | O | M | I | L | K | Q | T | A |
| U | A | L | Q | V | A | O | N | A | A | Z | E | U | S | D |
| D | D | I | A | N | A | R | O | S | S | I | Y | E | V | I |
| Y | O | U | N | G | K | I | R | K | T | F | L | E | A | O |
| K | I | R | S | T | Y | T | O | Y | S | T | O | R | Y | A |

1. RICHARD AND JUDY
2. ANDRE
3. WOGAN
4. RUSS
5. JONO
6. BREAKFAST
7. TOY STORY
8. NOLAN
9. KIRK
10. DIANA ROSS
11. VIRGIN RADIO
12. MASK
13. JIMMY
14. HARRY
15. HILL
16. YOKO ONO
17. SKY
18. MAD FOR IT
19. LIAM
20. CHIP
21. BOARD
22. QUEER
23. ZEUS
24. MILK
25. 'NICE PAD'
26. NEIL
27. KIRSTY
28. YOUNG
29. FLEA
30. RSZXIPIQ

**DESIGNED BY COMPUTER, USED BY IDIOTS**

**LOTS OF EXTRA BOOT SPACE**

**FULLY APPLE COMPATIBLE – OTHER FRUITS TO FOLLOW**

# COMPU-TABLE

## RUSS & JONO'S
## HOUSE OF CRAP

**START YOUR OWN MULTI-MILLION-POUND COMPUTER BUSINESS WITH THE ORIGINAL AND BEST . . . COMPU-TABLE**

Have you been missing out on the computer revolution? Have you watched as others have made micro-chip millions around you? Have you thought that if only you could get hold of the right equipment you could make millions too?

Finally the gear you've been waiting for is on the market (while stocks last) – the Russ & Jono Compu-table. Ergonomically designed by egg-heads at our top-secret research laboratory in the San Fernando Hills, it's the all-round computer solution that will help you make MILLIONS. Whether it be for home or office use the COMPU-TABLE will enable you to process megabytes of information in comfort and security.

It's easy to operate too – a child could do it – and has none of those awkward moving parts that can get in the way of you and your computing. Made of the highest quality poly-fibre chipboard™ you can put it up almost anywhere in seconds and get on with the job you need it for.

## NO WIRES . . .
## NO TIME WASTING . . .
## NO EXPENSIVE EXTRAS . . .
## NO WORRIES

So just don't just sit there with the wrong equipment. Get into the top flight with the desk of the future. Buy COMPU-TABLE . . . and start making big money.

Phone Basingstoke 009 and ask for Jim in Sales. He'll see you right.

COMPU-TABLE is available in a range of colours – grey, black and charcoal.

RUSS & JONO'S
# HOUSE OF CRAP
PRESENT

# CELLULIGHT

*Tired of using a shoe horn to put your jeans on?*
*Are you the butt of people's jokes?*
*Tired of all the wonder diets but nothing works?*

**BEFORE**

**After 1 week**

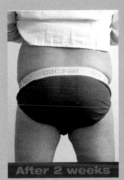

**After 2 weeks**

**After 4 weeks**

'Cellulight' is a wonder of the 20th century made from ancient herbs – and many by-products of the petro-chemical and livestock industries. It's completely harmless if used as directed and applied with the easy-care lead spatula (warning: never reuse applicator to serve babies' meals). It's a no-fuss product for today's busy lifestyle.

Well, you sound pretty easily sold when it comes to rubbish. Help is at hand with Russ & Jono's miracle treatment, 'Cellulight'. After only four weeks* of treatment just look at the difference . . . the weight simply falls off (and in some cases blisters and itches). No one, absolutely no one, is too fat to benefit from 'Cellulight'.

It worked for Jono and it can really work for you! Or your money back (sort of).

**Scientifically Tested**
Just follow the instructions and massage 'Cellulight' over the affected area and watch the pounds fall off – it's as simple as that (in most cases*).

After four weeks, get ready to worship the new you in front of your mirror in the bathroom.

*(\* May vary wildly depending on strength of chemicals.)*

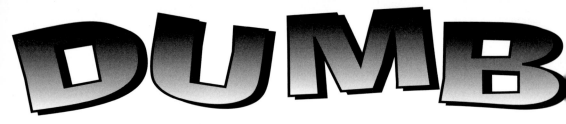

# DUMB

A raider who tried to hold up a butcher's shop in the Bronx (EDITOR'S NOTE: Do they have butcher's shops in the Bronx ? What do they sell? Best end of dead tourist?) accidentally shot himself in the foot during a fight with the owner, who then lassoed him with a string of sausages and locked him into the cold store until the Police arrived. The Police later confirmed that the raider was 'OK but was suffering from a number of deep cold cuts.'

In most States in the USA the legal drinking age is 21. It's pretty understandable therefore that thirsty teenager Scott West from Ohio would try his luck in a local liquor store with someone else's ID. Unfortunately the ID in question belonged to the guy behind the counter who had it stolen the week before. Poor young Scott was in such a hurry to get out of the store that he left his wallet – containing his genuine ID – behind and was arrested later on that day – stone-cold sober.

SHIVER!

# CRIMES

An enterprising car thief took desperate measures when cornered by police in Swindon — he hid in a garden shed with a lamp shade over his head. Unfortunately a man with an old rose-patterned lamp shade coming out of the top of his cranium doesn't exactly blend in with a load of rusting garden tools and a wheelbarrow. The police arrested the man and charged him with both theft and with being far too surreal for Swindon.

Two former jailbirds missed their convict buddies so much that they broke back IN to see them. The two men had been released from the prison in Adelaide, Australia only the day before when they climbed over the wall with a woman to have a midnight party in the cells. Unfortunately the partying caused the alarm to be raised, revealing the puzzling fact that the jail had too many prisoners. All three were later caught and charged, an act which sent the two men back inside legally — for parole violation.

A husband and wife bank robbery team, Dan and Sandra Golding, were arrested when police became suspicious about the seven-year-old girl at the wheel of a car parked outside the Malibu branch of Chemical bank. In a confession that will touch the hearts of parents everywhere the hapless robbers later said, 'We always take little Liza-May with us when we pull a job 'cos she always gets a big thrill out of pretending she's the getaway driver. Besides, it sure saves all that money and hassle of getting a baby-sitter who can drive and shoot at the same time.'

# Internet *Quiz*

All around the globe, people of all shapes and sizes are trading in their CB radios and trainspotting manuals and hooking up to the Internet. It's the biggest thing since sliced bread (whatever that's supposed to mean). But what is it? How does it work? How can you get on the Information Superhighway without getting stuck in a ten-mile tailback behind a caravan and a Portuguese lorry with a dodgy exhaust?

From the high-tech headquarters of Russ and Jono's throbbing broadcasting empire, we've commissioned a top team of software experts to create a virtual Internet tuition tool. This unique semi-computerised electronic teacher will lead you through the quagmire of ISDN, MSN, CNN, and BILLNBEN – and put you straight in the cyber fast lane!

Our unique Virtual Internet Tool will test your knowledge of Internet technology, in a virtual Internet environment, just like a real Internet experience. It's just like using a real Internet 'web-site'. Except there's no porn on it.

## Getting connected!

1 Open the book flat at this page
2 Read the first question
3 Close the book before you have a chance to answer
4 Try unsuccessfully for ten minutes to open the book again
5 Swear
6 Open the book at the wrong page
7 Close book
8 Swear again
9 Repeat steps 1–8 as many times as it takes for you to get really irritated
10 Take some valium, then prepare for the quiz!

## Using the web page!

1 Firmly grasp a perpendicular page-marking ink dispenser*
2 Decide on the correct answer
3 Mark the relevant box, whilst making a small 'beeping' sound
4 Read the next question, whilst making irritating keyboard 'tapping' sounds
5 Repeat 2–4 until quiz is finished
6 Repeat entire 'Getting Connected' section at least two more times

## Signing off

1 Stab the book repeatedly with your perpendicular page-marking ink dispenser
2 Throw it out the window
3 Get down the pub and drink yourself into a coma

(* pen)

# Here we go, surf-dudes!

Question 1 – What is the Internet?
- **a** A world-wide electronic computer information network
- **b** Where AC Milan try to put the ball in a local Derby against their Milanese rivals
- **c** European fish-quota agreement

Question 2 – Why should I get connected?
- **a** To communicate through the miracle of E-mail
- **b** To tap into a vast repository of international knowledge
- **c** To download the best porn you'll ever see outside of an Amsterdam hard-core sex shop

Question 3 – Does it cost much to be on the Internet?
- **a** Depends how long you're on line
- **b** Depends what you want to download
- **c** Depends on whether you get caught by your mum – keyboard in one hand, Internet tool in the other

Question 4 – What sort of people will I meet online?
- **a** Fun-loving, intelligent conversationalists
- **b** Cool netties living at the cutting edge of social technology
- **c** Look in the mirror, gitty. There's four million saddies just like you and none of them have friends

Question 5 – What's a bulletin board?
- **a** An electronic noticeboard for the exchange of ideas
- **b** A virtual world where like-minded netties can converse in a public forum
- **c** A one-way ticket to masturbation heaven

Question 6 – What's masturbation?
**Space error.**
**Click here to go to rest of quiz**

**Answers:** To check your answers to the quiz, go to our virtual Internet real Internet web site. www.russ&jono/quiz/answers/ questions/crap/houseofcrap/bollocks/ pussy2.html

# Sad but True

As our esteemed Prime Minister once remarked when talking about roadside toilet facilities 'when they've got to go, they've got to go' and boy did Trini Kallam have to go when he stopped his car in the Indonesian jungle to water the fauna. Tragically for the desperate motorist his improvised version of the Watford Gap services was not well chosen. He'd parked up only fifty yards from a hungry tigress who promptly leapt out of the bushes and ate him. But don't worry. Such things happen only very rarely on British roads. Even when John Major's in charge.

Remember. Death can come when you least expect it . . . seize the day . . .' So ran the theme of a lecture given on the subject of preparing for death being given by American author Todd Horton . . . or at least so would have run the lecture had not Mr Horton suffered a massive heart-attack and died right in the middle of his speech. The author, an expert on the legal and financial arrangements necessary to make death as easy as possible for the surviving relatives, naturally passed away without having any of his affairs in order or a properly signed will.

When you've got to go – go in style. So ran the last words of Spanish retired cake shop owner Emilio Formar, whose death was meant to result in a quietly dignified family funeral. Imagine the horror of his widow when she discovered that, in order to make the un-Spanishly tall *Señor* Formar fit into the left-over coffin they intended to use at his cremation, unscrupulous undertakers had sawn off his head and jammed it between his legs. Their later attempts to argue that this was an ancient practice much used on mediaeval kings did not go down very well.

Venezuelan businessman Raul Santa enjoyed his little fishing trips to the Amazon. They provided a relaxing break from a busy life in the city, a chance to get in touch with himself and with nature. Unfortunately for Raul the contact became all too real one weekend when his line became entangled in an overhanging tree. His furious attempts to shake the hook free only succeeded in waking up a swarm of killer bees which promptly set upon him with a vengeance. Raul did the sensible thing and leapt into the river itself – whereupon he was eaten alive by a shoal of hungry piranhas. What a sad, sad story. Correct me if I'm wrong but doesn't Chris Tarrant like to go fishing? Now, where exactly is the Amazon again?

The life of an Italian chef is not an easy one, not only because of the great heat and the volatile customers but because of the dirty tricks the ingredients can play on you. Maybe Gerio Pangelli should have been better prepared for the fatal attack of thirty-odd strands of uncooked spaghetti which impaled him in the chest when a surprise 120 mph gust of wind blew off the Mediterranean into his kitchen . . . but then again, maybe not. After all, isn't pasta supposed to be good for the heart?

# Spicy Story

There's more to being a DJ than entertaining a nation with your natural charm, verbal humour and fantastic musical taste. We're also benevolent icons of our industry, seeking out new talent and encouraging promising acts.

Did you know, for instance, that we are solely responsible for the massive world-wide success of the Spice Girls? We discovered them!

That's right. In the early seventies, while we were developing the format of our hugely successful *Breakfast Experience*, we staggered into a cocktail bar in Melbourne and witnessed the future of pop. They were five gorgeous waitresses when we saw them. We picked them up and turned them around – in more ways than one! In fact we turned them into something new. We turned them into THE SPICE GIRLS.

They weren't called the Spice Girls way back then. They were the Herb Birds. There was Garden Herb, Dried Herb, Mixed Herb, French Herb (she preferred Herb de Provence) and Herb-Peas (bit of a sore

point, that name. It proved tricky to get rid of). In their tight-fitting hot-pants and sequin boob tubes we saw enormous potential, and signed them up to a fifty year management contract on the spot. Of course, the acne's nearly all cleared up now, so it's difficult to say which spot it was it was, but it was big enough for us all to write our names on, which is all that's needed really. Years later we accused Scary Spice of putting the squeeze on our contract, but that's another story.

After managing a long and successful club career including two summer spells in Blackpool and an Armed Forces gig on the Falkland Islands, we secured them a contract dubbing the songs in a number of feature films, including timeless classics such as *Hello Dolly*, *The Sound of Music*, *The Exorcist* and *Teletubbies – The Movie*. Secrecy was imperative – we wanted to keep their true identity hidden until the world was ready for Girl Power, a new and exciting political ideology developed by the girls after listening to the insane rantings of their Great Uncle Karl (that's Mr Marx to you and I). He was actually the original Tinky Winky Tubby. (Another exclusive, folks.)

The group decided to stretch out in the early 1990s and enter the film industry. Unfortunately a little-known Hollywood law forbids anyone without a penis working in those kind of movies. So they paid a man from their local video store to 'front' the production of two long-forgotten scripts that the girls had written on tour during the 1950s. The titles were Long Shlong Saliva and Deep Throat Girl Power on Heat. The girls decided to go public with their act and gain the international stardom we all felt they deserved. For their first singe we chose 'Wannabe' – a catchy ditty which Baby Spice used to perform with her mother (Barbara Windsor) at the height of the Victorian variety music hall craze. The movies were cult and buck's party hits and still available today from the Sunday Sport video club.

The rest, as they say, is history.

The next chapter of the Spice Girls saga is yet to be written, but we can reveal a secret which even their record company doesn't know. Pictured with us here is Richard (Big Boy) Branson, the man who made Virgin what it is today. (As a note of interest, the reason Richard rushed to sign us up on Virgin Radio was the repayment of an old debt. We lent him the money to buy his first aeroplane-cum-houseboat, and so he returned the favour by giving us our own radio station. Cool huh!)

So what's the connection with the Spice Girls, we hear you cry? Well, although it has yet to be announced, we have negotiated Richard's entry (don't tell his

wife) into this pop sensation. Richard begged on his hands and knees to be a Spice Girl, and after a chat with the girls themselves, we convinced them it was just the right move for this stage of their career. (The six-figure cash sum helped too.)

So next time you watch *Top of the Pops*, forget Scary Spice, Baby Spice, Sporty Spice, Posh Spice and Ginger Spice. It's the new Hairy Spice you want to watch for. She'll be making pop history!

Russ and I spend a lot of time with the girls during our crazy showbiz lifestyles. But we draw the line at trimming Hairy Spice's beard line.

And that's OFFICIAL.

# Probe the

Yu Chen Yu — Taiwan's very own answer to Trevor McDonald — shocked the nation when he announced on the 1 p.m. news that his wife of 14 years had left him for another man. The distraught TV presenter then burst into tears, produced a .45 calibre revolver from his inside pocket and shot himself dead on screen. Unfortunately, Jeremy Paxman is not married . . . nor is he ever likely to be.

Americans take the question of their future very seriously. Small wonder that a 52 year-old Minnesota woman was so unhappy when numerous fortune-tellers kept looking at her palm and predicting a short and miserable life that she paid a plastic surgeon $10,000 to change it. Working to the most basic principles of palmistry that states that a short and broken life line indicates a short and broken life, super-superstitious Helen Sanger had a much longer and straighter one created instead. As she said later 'Palmists used to be too embarrassed to read my hand. Now they can't say enough about what a wonderful future I have.' And Americans have the nerve to say that Colonel Gaddafi is barking mad.

Death American style is never straightforward. At least that must be the sole comforting thought for the mourners at the funeral of pizza tycoon Patrick Maseo whose final request before he departed for that great deep-pan factory in the sky was that his ashes be spread on an enormous pizza and fed to the guests at the funeral. Shocked guests bravely munched their way though the gruesome feast washing good old Pat down with gallons of coke and a side-order of garlic bread. One mourner was so happy he actually went back for seconds claiming it was the best pizza he'd eaten in years but then again Hannibal Lecter did come from the difficult side of the family.

# Globe

Singapore is a very strict society that still includes caning and execution amongst its common list of punishments. All the more incredible that convicted killer John Wu has been on death row there for . . . 27 years – all thanks to the fact that he refuses to pick his last meal. Wu is exploiting a loophole in Singapore law that means he cannot be hanged until all the formalities – including choosing and eating his final repast – have been met. As a result Woo has either turned down whatever is offered to him or said he's too sick to eat the best gourmet grub Singapore can offer. And though the authorities know full well what Woo's up to there's not a single thing they can do about it. The same rule will not apply to Nick Leeson should he return to face the music on the quite reasonable grounds that bankers don't have any human rights and deserve to die as quickly as possible.

Weddings can often be wild and crazy events that spin out of control. This is particularly true in the Peshawar region of Pakistan where, not content with tossing a box of confetti or tying condoms to the groom's car aerial, male guests have taken to firing rifles in the air in celebration. Fair enough you might say except if you happened to have been at the nuptial celebration where the firing was so intense that not only was the bride's father killed by a stray bullet but electrical power lines were severed, setting the whole village on fire. In justification for their acts one of the guests commented 'If I do not use my gun when invited to a wedding, I will be considered a mouse.' Or indeed a man with an incredibly small penis.

# EXCLUSIVE!!! MY LIFE AS A WOMAN

## Wacky DJ Spends 2 Years as SEX slave in seedy London Massage Parlour

**BY *NEWS OF THE SCREWS* REPORTERS**

Aussie breakfast DJ sensation Jonathan Coleman, heavyweight half of the successful Russ and Jono duo, today revealed a sordid sexual past as a sex slave in a North London massage parlour called 'The Soft Touch'. The revelation came after pictures of the hunky DJ in action were printed EXCLUSIVELY by the *News Of The Screws* last Sunday causing a storm of outrage in newsrooms up and down the country.

At last, after six months of extensive investigation by star undercover reporter Suzzie Sleaze, the whole story behind these horrendous pictures is ready to be told as we prove beyond a shadow of a doubt that Coleman massaged over 25 top people – including MPs, Bishops and members of the Rambling Association – during an eight-month period as a woman in 1990.

Though at first Coleman denied the allegations the evidence gathered by our reporters – including signed statements, video footage, massage-oil samples and secret audio tapes recorded with microphones hidden inside bodily orifices – proved too much for him and he was forced to issue a statement through top showbiz lawyer Nick Schlong.

'At first this strange episode totally slipped Mr Coleman's mind. Now, thanks mainly to six months of intensive ego workshops and electric shock therapy

at the Anneka Rice Clinic in Harlow, he now has a vague memory of something like this happening. Mr Coleman was suffering acute dislocation depression as a result of the trauma of hosting a BBC1 morning quiz called *Humdingers* which proved so traumatic to my client that he can even now not refer to the series in question by name. When you add this into the emotional strain of working on BBC1's *Hit The Road* and a series of failed media relationships with Annabel Giles and Dr Hilary, the result was cataclysmic. Mr Coleman deeply regrets what happened, particularly his choice of lingerie and wishes to assure fans he will stick to silk in future.'

Coleman's radio partner Russ Williams was too shocked to comment at the £560,000 North London home he shares with his young Korean assistant Kim Sue Kim, though his manager Aaron Spielberg of Oi Vay Inc was more forthcoming. 'Russ and Jono's relationship has only ever been a professional one. They don't see each other socially and my boy has never had any inkling of Jono's former life, apart from one time when Russ had a bad back and Jono whipped out his oil and fixed it, in a jiffy. At no time in the above matter did Jono offer nor Russ accept any so-called special services other than those

you might expect between two radio colleagues in an enclosed studio. Russ is deeply upset by the whole thing – so much so in fact that he has contacted police with information relating to the theft of extra large sizes from a number of womenswear shops near the Virgin studios in London.'

Virgin supremo Richard Branson was unavailable for comment though an insider said that 'Richard actually quite likes the photos and didn't realise Jono had such nice legs when he hired him. Actually he's now thinking of using Jono to help launch a new top secret Virgin drink next year that's being developed especially for the transsexual market code named 'Blush'.

Last night as he left his London flat with a coat over his head the rotunder from down under refused to add to his lawyer's statement, though when asked if he was still a cross-dresser fumed 'Listen mate. If you had to get up at 4.30 every morning you'd be a f****ing cross dresser too.'

# DUMB

Nikolai Swechtz, a Bulgarian jewel thief, was so keen to avoid being caught red-handed by police with a load of stolen necklaces that he swallowed them ... and nearly choked to death. As doctors struggled to save him police were optimistic of their chances of recovering the missing goods. 'It will all come out in court' said a spokesman.'

As Dale Winton knows only too well, it's amazing what you can get away with if you're on TV. Even Dale, though, wouldn't have pushed his luck as far as Dieter Langenhoffen from Frankfurt, an enterprising lad who stole over £700 by going round to drinkers in a bar with a sign saying 'Candid Camera – Please Co-Operate' and taking money out of people's wallets and purses in front of their very noses. The punters, believing they were being filmed by a hidden camera, happily obliged and just grinned inanely as Dieter walked off with their hard-earned Deutschmarks. Unfortunately, Dieter's TV career proved to be even shorter than Danny Baker's when, trying his Candid Camera trick a week later, he was nicked by a squad of Candid Policemen.

Ray Leggit, a first-time bank robber from Perth, Australia, showed that the master criminals' arts don't come naturally to everyone when he tried to rob a post office disguised in a motorbike helmet that had his name printed on it in large silver letters.

# CRIMES

Some people just can't do anything without bringing their bloody kids along, eh? They bring them to restaurants, they bring them to weddings, they even bring them to shoplifting sprees. Or at least that's what bungling thief Geoff Armes did when he went along to his local DIY Superstore to nick himself a power drill and accessories with his baby daughter Holly in tow. Cleverly spotting the potential of the pram Geoff set his daughter to one side, tucked a large Black & Decker under the blankets and, everything back in place, headed for the exits. All was going totally to plan till, just as he reached the front door, he realised he had left Holly behind on a shelf full of masonry bits and that she was screaming blue murder. Before he could do anything else a kindly security guard rushed up with his darling daughter ... and pulled back the covers to put her in the pram. By the time the police arrived both Geoff and Holly were bawling their eyes out.

John Dingle thought he had committed the perfect crime when, high on a cocktail of drugs and Tia Maria, he broke into his local sweet shop and got away with two packets of Rollos and a jar of bullseyes. Naturally, he was shocked to wake up to find the police at the foot of his bed. His astonishment at the sharp work of the boys in blue was somewhat muted when he realised it had been snowing that night and Plod had simply followed the tracks in the snow all the way from the sweet shop to his own front door – sixty yards up the street.

# Celebrity

Noddy Holder

Vanessa Feltz hanging
around Russ

Richard E Grant

# Gallery

*An early morning fiddle with Vanessa Mae*

Richard O'Brien

Les Dennis

Sean Hughes

Caprice

Bill Oddie

# RUSS & JONO'S HOUSE OF CRAP PRESENTS

## *A spiritual journey to your hidden self, through the joys of a*

# *Healing Weekend*

**L**ife may be a laugh-a-minute non-stop roller-coaster ride of shag-festing and party-going for some people, but for most of us it's a downright miserable ride on a Number 7 bus with someone smelly next to us and our raincoat making the seat damp.

At Russ & Jono's House of Crap we understand what it's like to be one of life's losers. Actually, we know what it's like to be two of life's losers. Contrary to public opinion, we didn't become the world's greatest living DJs through our extraordinary wit and razor tongues. No! We hit the bigtime because we got in touch with our inner selves. We healed the divide between our vastly inflated egos, and our pitifully low public esteem.

And now this inner peace can be yours, thanks to the works of Jonai Lama and Russo Maharajah – two of the world's leading spiritual advisers and tax-evasion consultants. Millions around the world have discovered emotional harmony using the teachings of these remarkable gurus (the millions in question now reside in numbered offshore bank accounts).

Through an exclusive licensing agreement with Russ & Jono's House of Crap, you too can enjoy the benefits of lighter souls, thinner wallets and well-moisturised skin at our all-inclusive Healing Weekend.

But don't take our word for it. Hear what the rich and famous have to say!

*'Jonai Lama changed my life. I'm not sure who changed my underwear.'*

Sporty Spice

*'They have so much to teach, and I have so much to learn. Isn't Jonai Lama a rugby player?'*

Johnny Ball

*'Nice neighbours'*

George Harrison

*'I'm sorry, I really don't have a clue what you're talking about. Stop phoning me.'*

Richard Madeley

## THE WORKSHOPS

Upon your arrival at Winton Hall you will slide off the shackles of your pitiful, grubby little lives and enter an oasis of tranquillity and personal discovery. Our series of workshops are individually tailored to expose (and then cure!) your deep neuroses and irrational sexual hang-ups. Guests are reminded that all they need bring is their Gold Amex card, some loose, see-through clothing and at least two bottles of scented baby oil. The taking of photographs is strictly forbidden, as we do enough of that ourselves.

### Fumbling in the Dark

Relive the heady excitement of your first teenage sexual experience as we bundle you in the back of a Ford Capri and let you make out in the dark. Get caught by 'irate parents' for a small additional fee. Useful intro for the 'Got My Girfriend Pregnant And Buggered Up My Life' group discussions.

### Survivor's Survivors Course

Are you dealing with rage and anger at being forced to deal with your rage and anger? Bitten off more than you can chew? Try the survivor's survivors course. Guest speakers Michael Tyson and Gloria Gaynor.

### Colonic Irrigation

You'll never find equilibrium or inner peace if your plumbing's bunged up. Colonic Irrigation is this year's in (and then swiftly out again) thing. Our expert practitioners have many years of experience, some having formerly been operatives with Dyno-Rod, and use specially designed equipment culled from top of the range domestic appliances. Delightfully refreshing.

### Mumbo Jumbo Hippy Dogma

Light the joss stick, man. Skin up and chill out. Like, don't hurt the trees, right? Oh man, it's so obvious, build more roads and more people will drive cars. Er, Thai I think.

---

*ABOUT OUR WORLD FAMOUS FACILITATORS*

#### Russo Maharajah

*Raised by Tibetan monks after being mysteriously abandoned as a baby, Russo Maharajah is a pupil of Sri Hi-Bran, the ancient Eastern mystic. Now a Yogi Bear Master and papercut warrior in his own right, he has been taught in the mysterious ways of the love-goddess Culdesac. He lives only that he may share this knowledge with his disciples (brunettes preferred).*

#### Jonai Lama

*The legendary figure of Jonai Lama is roundly recognised as the driving force behind the resurgence of New Age philosophy. He's more usually recognised as the driving force behind the wheel of one of his 178 vintage Rolls Royces. These he has acquired as an ironic symbol of the world left behind in search of spiritual happiness.*

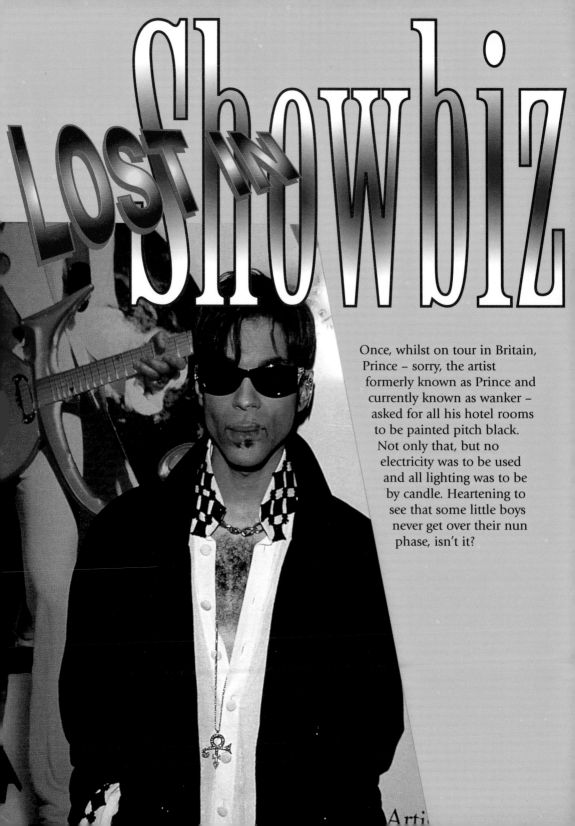

# Lost in Showbiz

Once, whilst on tour in Britain, Prince – sorry, the artist formerly known as Prince and currently known as wanker – asked for all his hotel rooms to be painted pitch black. Not only that, but no electricity was to be used and all lighting was to be by candle. Heartening to see that some little boys never get over their nun phase, isn't it?

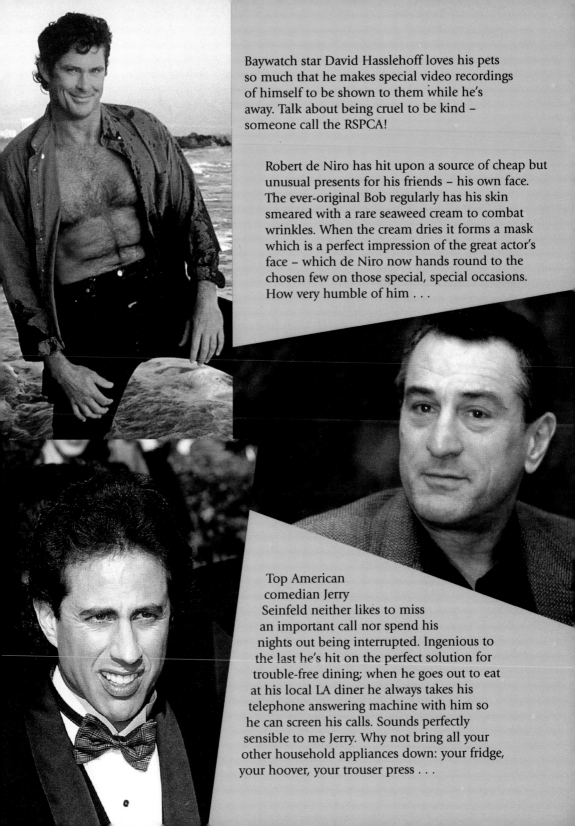

Baywatch star David Hasslehoff loves his pets so much that he makes special video recordings of himself to be shown to them while he's away. Talk about being cruel to be kind – someone call the RSPCA!

Robert de Niro has hit upon a source of cheap but unusual presents for his friends – his own face. The ever-original Bob regularly has his skin smeared with a rare seaweed cream to combat wrinkles. When the cream dries it forms a mask which is a perfect impression of the great actor's face – which de Niro now hands round to the chosen few on those special, special occasions. How very humble of him . . .

Top American comedian Jerry Seinfeld neither likes to miss an important call nor spend his nights out being interrupted. Ingenious to the last he's hit on the perfect solution for trouble-free dining; when he goes out to eat at his local LA diner he always takes his telephone answering machine with him so he can screen his calls. Sounds perfectly sensible to me Jerry. Why not bring all your other household appliances down: your fridge, your hoover, your trouser press . . .

# That's My Boy

## A TIPTOE THROUGH
## MRS PATRICIA PRIMROSE WILLIAMS' PHOTO ALBUM

———

Russ was born into this world on the 21st of January 19 hundred and 62. It was a Wednesday I think. The weather was a little cold and damp in the morning though it did freshen up nicely after *Wagonners' Walk*. I don't know why, call me psychic, but as soon as I got up that morning I just knew that today I was going to have a baby – which was doubly strange as at that moment I didn't even know I was pregnant. After all, there have been cases of indigestion that lasted nine months before, surely?

Anyway, whatever the moral rights and wrongs, around four o'clock that afternoon I came over all queer at the launderette and had to be revived with a nice cup of Typhoo and a couple of thick slices of Battenburg. Three hours later little Russ came into this world, naked but for his Spurs scarf and a large rosette with Glenn Hoddle's face on it. He didn't scream when the midwife slapped his bottom, only when she stopped. Babies can be strange creatures sometimes.

From the start Russ stood out from the crowd. He was always cheerful, friendly and immensely self-confident – though his habit of leaning out of his pram and handing out signed pictures of himself was a bit of a nuisance when I was trying to scoot round Spar and get back in time for *Pebble Mill*. Unfortunately I missed Russ's first words as I was upstairs in the bedroom at the time having a private chat with that nice, handsome washing machine man but I'm sure they were as funny as he said they were.

Time flies by when you've got a baby to look after and so many catalogues to study and suddenly one day I looked up from the Green Shield Stamps' hostess trolley selection to find him dressed and ready to go to school. Unfortunately this was on a Sunday in August so he had a little longer before he could turn the sandpit into a no-fly zone and start teaching his classmates to look out for the smutty bits in *Captain Pugwash*.

Russ loved his holidays, especially those happy, happy weeks at Blackpool when he had so much fun pouring boiling oil down from the turret of his impregnable sand castles and